A Short History of Polar Exploration

D0892801

Other Pocket Essentials by Nick Rennison

Sigmund Freud
Peter Mark Roget: The Man Who Became a Book
Robin Hood: History, Myth, Culture

A
Short History
of Polar Exploration

NICK RENNISON

POCKET ESSENTIALS

First published in 2013 by Pocket Essentials,
an imprint of Oldcastle Books Ltd,
PO Box 394, Harpenden,
Herts, AL5 1XJ
www.pocketessentials.com

A CIP catalogue record for this book is available from the British Library.

ISBN
978-1-84344-090-1 (print)
978-1-84344-091-8 (kindle)
978-1-84343-092-5 (epub)
978-1-84344-093-2 (pdf)

2 4 6 8 10 9 7 5 3 1

Typeset by Avocet Typeset, Somerton, Somerset
in 9.75pt Univers Light
Printed and bound in Great Britain by Clays Ltd, St Ives plc

'Polar exploration is at once the cleanest and most isolated way of having a bad time which has been devised.'

Apsley Cherry-Garrard

'We led a strange, weird sort of life. A spice of danger, with much of beauty and a world of magnificence.'

Isaac Israel Hayes

Acknowledgements

My first thanks must go to Ion Mills at Pocket Essentials who commissioned me to write a short history of a subject in which I have long been interested and thus allowed me to revisit the fascinating stories of Scott and Amundsen, the disappearance of Sir John Franklin and his men, and all the other tales that make the discovery of new territory in the Arctic and Antarctica such a gripping chapter in the history of exploration. Thanks also to Claire Watts who patiently and efficiently guided the book towards publication in record time. Jayne Lewis for her copy-editing skills, Alan Forster created a brilliant and eye-catching cover, Richard Howard worked long hours at short notice on the index, as did Paul Medcalf in typesetting the book. I am grateful to all of them. Amongst friends and family, my thanks go particularly to Kevin Chappell, Anita Diaz, Cindy Rennison, Eileen Rennison, John Thewlis and Wolfgang Lüers who have all, at one time or another, listened sympathetically as I have spoken, at greater length than they probably expected, on the subject of polar exploration. My final thanks must, as always, go to my wife Eve who has been wonderfully supportive and helpful throughout my work on this book.

Contents

Introduction

The Arctic and the Antarctic have been the settings for some of the most compelling dramas in the history of exploration. Some are very well known. Scott making his desperate bid to return to safety after being pre-empted at the South Pole by Amundsen and dying in a blizzard just eleven miles short of supplies at One Ton Depot. Sir John Franklin and the men with him disappearing into the Canadian Arctic in search of the Northwest Passage, never to be seen alive again. Shackleton undertaking an epic boat journey across the Antarctic seas to South Georgia in order to bring help to his men stranded on the uninhabited Elephant Island. Others, like Douglas Mawson's solo trek to his Antarctic home base after the death of his two companions or Greely's disastrous expedition in the Arctic which led to the deaths of most of its members and accusations of cannibalism levelled at the survivors, are less familiar.

This book attempts a brief survey of the larger story in which these dramatic incidents take their place. It contains a few introductory pages to the history of attempts to locate either a Northwest Passage or a Northeast Passage from the Atlantic to the Pacific in the centuries between the mariners of the Elizabethan Age and the navigators who were Captain Cook's contemporaries. It also includes the shortest of guides to the long-standing idea of *Terra Australis* and Cook's demonstration that no such continent, as it had been thought to exist – temperate and well-populated – could possibly lie in the waters of the Far South. However, most of it concentrates on the 140 years between 1820 and 1960. At the beginning of this period, the Antarctic continent had only just been sighted for the first time and much of the geography of the Canadian and Russian Arctic remained a mystery. At the end of it, there were no more blanks on the maps at either end of the earth and scientists and even tourists were just as likely to be found there as explorers and adventurers. The first six chapters of *A Short History of Polar Exploration* tell the story of these 140 years. They are followed by a very short chapter on the poles in the last fifty years and one on the role the poles have played in literature and the arts for two centuries. The brief biographical dictionary of polar explorers provides a reference guide to the characters who created the dramas of Arctic and Antarctic exploration. The book ends with a bibliography which guides anyone who is interested to books that can reveal far more about polar history than I can hope to do in these pages. If this 'short history' arouses interest in what is an extraordinary story populated by extraordinary people, it will have done its job.

The Arctic Pre-1900

Before 1800

For centuries men entered the North American Arctic not in the hopes of reaching the pole but in quest for what became a Holy Grail of maritime navigation – the Northwest Passage. Somewhere in the wastelands of ice and sea there was, they believed, a navigable route from Atlantic to Pacific. This Northwest Passage, if only it could be found, would open up a new avenue to the riches of Asia. In search of it, the early explorers of the Arctic endured terrible hardships and many of them lost their lives.

The very first expeditions were English. Martin Frobisher was the archetypal Elizabethan seadog – daring, independent and bloody-minded – and he was one of those captains who fought off the Spanish Armada in 1588. He was also an intrepid, if slightly deluded, explorer of the Canadian Arctic. In 1576, backed by the Muscovy Company of London merchants, he sailed north-west and eventually landed on what is now Baffin Island. After an assortment of misadventures, including the capture of some of his men by a group of native people, he returned home, carrying samples of a black rock which, Frobisher was firmly convinced, contained gold enough to justify the despatch of further expeditions. Investors, including the Queen, agreed with him and he led two further journeys to the region. He brought back close to 1500 tons of the mysterious ore but, despite all Frobisher's hopes for it, it proved almost entirely worthless.

None the less, other English mariners followed in Frobisher's wake. Sir Humphrey Gilbert, who was Sir Walter Raleigh's half-brother and had written an influential treatise on 'a new passage to Cathay' in the 1570s, sailed for Newfoundland in 1583 and took possession of it for Elizabeth I. On his way back home, the ship on which he was sailing went down and all on board drowned. John Davis, like Gilbert a Devon man, undertook a series of voyages in the late 1580s to the strait west of Greenland which now bears his name. Perhaps most significantly, Henry Hudson made four journeys into Arctic waters from 1607 onwards, acting on behalf of companies of London merchants in search of a new commercial route. On the last of his voyages, in 1610, he entered the bay now named after him and he and his men were forced by the ice to winter on shore. In the spring of the following year, the captain was eager to explore his bay further but most of the sailors with him were less enthusiastic about the prospect. Cold, miserable and frightened, they just wanted to go home. They mutinied and forced Hudson, his son and a few loyal crewmen into a small boat which was then set adrift. The occupants of the small boat were never seen again. The mutineers returned to London where they admitted what they had done but put the blame on two ringleaders who had conveniently died on the voyage home. Some of the survivors were put on trial but acquitted.

Meanwhile other explorers from other nations were looking for a Northeast Passage that would take them across the top of Europe and down into the Pacific. In the 1590s, the Dutchman Willem Barents undertook three voyages to the Arctic Ocean. On the third of them, he and his men not only made the first indisputable sighting of the island of Spitsbergen but also became the first Western Europeans to survive a winter in the high Arctic. Others followed occasionally in their wake in the seventeenth century but it was not until the 1720s that the Danish-born Vitus Bering, serving in the Russian navy and approaching Arctic waters from the Pacific rather than the Baltic, sailed through the strait that now bears his name. On a second voyage in 1741, Bering made further important discoveries and sighted the southern coast of Alaska but the expedition, struck by illness and sailing in uncharted waters, was soon in trouble. In December 1741, Bering himself died on a remote island, now also named after him. The survivors of his expedition reached safety eight months later.

Hopes of finding a Northwest Passage had not died with Henry Hudson. A few years after he had met his fate, another English navigator, William Baffin, was despatched by London merchants in search of it. In 1616, sailing to the west of Greenland, he came upon the bay that now carries his name and charted it with exemplary thoroughness, naming straits that led off it Lancaster Sound, Jones Sound and Smith Sound after three of the men who had sent him. All three straits were to play a major role in future Arctic exploration. Fifteen years after Baffin's expedition, Luke Foxe, an experienced Yorkshire mariner, sailed north of Hudson Bay and entered the basin of water that is now called Foxe Basin. Ice-bound for most of the year, it none the less offered hopes of locating a Northwest Passage beyond Hudson Bay.

However, after Foxe's return, enthusiasm for exploration in the Far North dwindled. It was commerce rather than discovery which became the priority and the Hudson's Bay Company, founded in 1670, became the focus for fur trading in the vast region around the bay. It was to be another fifty years before anyone made any serious attempt to find a Northwest Passage and then it was to be a man who was very nearly an octogenarian. James Knight, born about 1640, had worked for the Hudson's Bay Company for decades when he began to look around for opportunities to verify rumours he had long heard about an easy and mineral-rich route through to the Pacific. In 1719, with two ships named the *Albany* and the *Discovery*, he set out to find it. Foreshadowing another, more famous expedition in the next century, he and his ships were never seen again. Debris from the ships was found and the remains of a camp on a remote island were located more than forty years later but the exact details of the fate of Knight and those with him remain a mystery.

Christopher Middleton was an English navigator who had worked as a ship's captain for the Hudson's Bay Company for many years. His interests in science and exploration were not shared by his employer unless they added to its profits and, in 1741, he took a commission in the Royal Navy in order to lead an Admiralty-sponsored expedition into the far north of Hudson Bay. After journeying to the edge of the Arctic Circle, Middleton found what seemed at first sight to be the entrance into a passage leading westwards and cheerfully named it Cape Hope. Unfortunately, it was no such thing and, after giving the stretch of water he had found the less cheerful name of Repulse Bay, he headed homewards. There he became embroiled in a bitter row with his major patron, the Anglo-Irish politician Arthur Dobbs. Middleton was now convinced that no Northwest Passage existed, at least not one with any outlet anywhere near where he had sailed in Hudson Bay. Dobbs thought that Middleton simply hadn't looked hard enough for it and decided to back another expedition which would be more thorough in its efforts. Led by William Moor, a cousin of Middleton who had sailed on the previous expedition and taken Dobbs's view of his relation's conscientiousness, this voyage was even less successful than its predecessor in finding any trace of what might be the body of water for which they were all searching.

By the 1760s it was clear that no Northwest Passage existed where the expeditions of the last few decades had been looking. 'I am certain and shure,' one senior employee of the Hudson's Bay Company wrote with a better grasp of geography than of conventional spelling, 'that there is no pasage into the Western Ocan in this Hudsons Bay.' One possibility, to which many optimists still clung, was that the entrance to the Passage was located further north than anyone had travelled. The other was that it would be easier to find a route from the Pacific to the Atlantic rather than vice versa. And, if anyone was going to be able to find such a route, it would surely be the man who was widely acclaimed as the greatest navigator of his day. Captain James Cook had already added enormously to the sum of human geographical knowledge in two voyages which had made him the first man to cross the Antarctic Circle and had more or less destroyed the credibility of old ideas about a temperate southern continent (*Terra Australis*), vast and well-populated, stretching across the bottom of the world. In July 1776, he was despatched on a third voyage which would, everybody at the Admiralty hoped, finally settle the question of the Northwest Passage. He was, according to his instructions, to head for the north Pacific, sail up the coast of north-west America to latitude 65° N and there 'to search for, and to explore, such rivers or inlets as may appear to be of a considerable extent, and pointing towards Hudsons or Baffins Bay'. With two ships, the *Resolution* under his own captaincy and the *Discovery*, commanded by Charles Clerke, Cook set out from Plymouth to fulfil these instructions.

After becoming the first Europeans to visit the Hawaiian islands at the beginning of 1778, Cook and his men sailed towards North America and began the job they had been given of mapping the coastline northwards. Over the next few months they made their way steadily up the coast to Alaska and the Bering Strait. Cook was keen to make headway through the Strait but the ships were turned back by ice several times. Eventually he retired to the Aleutian Islands where he made repairs to the *Resolution* and the *Discovery* and encountered some Russian fur traders. (The meeting was a frustrating one for both sides since the Russians spoke no English, Cook had no Russian speaker on his expedition and the limitations of sign language rapidly became apparent.) Once the ships were ready, he turned back south, intending to return to the region the following year. The voyage ended in tragedy when the

Resolution and the *Discovery* returned to Hawaii in 1779. Feted initially by the islanders, Cook left to continue his voyage but was forced back by damage to his ship and met with a very different welcome. For reasons still not entirely understood, the Hawaiians were now hostile and, in a confrontation with Cook and his men, they killed the great navigator. Clerke took charge of the expedition and it returned, as planned, to the American Northwest but the new commander was a sick man. After a final attempt on the Bering Strait, he died of tuberculosis in a harbour on the Kamchatka Peninsula. It was left to John Gore, who had sailed with Cook on his first voyage, to take the thoroughly demoralised expedition back to Britain.

Just as he had scotched any ideas about *Terra Australis*, Cook seemed to have destroyed any hopes that a passage to Hudson Bay or Baffin Bay could be found in the American Northwest but there were still lingering doubts and empty spaces on the map on to which some imaginative geographers could still project their dreams. One final expedition was needed to show conclusively that such dreams did not match reality. In the 1790s, George Vancouver, who had been a midshipman on Cook's second and third expeditions, undertook a voyage of several years which mapped the north-west coastline of America so skilfully that the charts he created were still being used more than a century later. He found plenty of inlets, bays and harbours but no sign of any passage that might lead all the way through to Hudson Bay or Baffin Bay in the east. 'I trust the precision with which the survey of the coast of North West America has been carried into effect,' Vancouver wrote, 'will remove every doubt, and set aside every opinion of a north-west passage.' For the moment it did, and the distractions of the long war with France that had just begun meant that journeys of discovery were largely forgotten, but the longstanding idea of a route between the two oceans stubbornly refused to die.

Ross, Parry and 'The Man Who Ate His Boots'

A new era in Arctic exploration dawned in the two decades after the defeat of Napoleon at Waterloo as a whole series of British expeditions was despatched northwards. The driving force behind them was Sir John Barrow who held the position of Second Secretary to the Admiralty for nearly forty years in the first half of the nineteenth century. Barrow had sailed on a whaling ship to the Arctic as a teenager in 1780 and travelled in such distant lands as China (where he was a member of the first British diplomatic mission to the country) and South Africa. After Napoleon's defeat in 1815 and his subsequent exile to St Helena (a place of retirement for the Emperor reportedly first suggested by Barrow), peace came to Europe for a generation. Naval officers no longer had the opportunities offered by war to forge successful careers. Barrow saw an alternative arena in which they could shine. Through exploring the unknown regions of the world, they could win the kind of fame and glory that their predecessors had gained in battle. And few lands were quite as unknown as those in the Far North.

The first of Barrow's new expeditions left London in April 1818 under the command of John Ross, a career officer who had joined the Navy in 1786 when he was aged only nine. Much of Ross's recent experience had been in Baltic waters, which was as close as any naval officer of the time had been to the Arctic, and this may have influenced Barrow in his choice. It was a choice which he was to come to regret, although Ross was to go on to have one of the most extensive Arctic careers of the century.

Sailing with two ships, the *Isabella* and the *Alexander*, Ross was instructed to sail into Baffin Bay and look for an outlet which might open into the Northwest Passage. His expedition had its minor successes. He made first contact with a group of Inuit who had never before seen white men. Indeed, they believed themselves to be the only people in the world and were much astonished by the appearance of Ross's men. He mapped areas of Baffin Bay that had never been previously mapped. However, his main task was to search for a Northwest Passage and, in that, he failed comprehensively. For reasons that have never been adequately explained, he seemed curiously prepared to accept, on slender evidence, that there was no way through the straits that led off Baffin Bay. Smith Sound and Jones Sound he swiftly dismissed as bays from which there could be no further passage northwards. Lancaster Sound, the third of the straits discovered by William Baffin two centuries earlier, was seen as the likeliest location of a passage that would lead eventually to the Pacific. In September 1818, Ross sailed into it and noted land on the horizon. He was convinced that what he saw was a mountain range and that it blocked any further attempt to travel up Lancaster Sound. Others on board his ships were not so sure. Some thought that what he had seen was a mirage, of the kind all too likely to trouble explorers in the Far North, and that he should have pressed on to make certain of his observations. The controversy that ensued when Ross returned to England was to blight both his career and his relations with many other names now famous in polar exploration.

In the wake of this unsatisfactory voyage, Barrow, who was more angered by Ross's incuriosity than anyone, planned further voyages by both land and sea to explore the Canadian Arctic and search for a Northwest Passage. For reasons that are not entirely clear, John Franklin, a career naval officer, was picked to lead the land expedition. A brave, charming but not very inspiring man who had fought as a teenager at the Battle of Trafalgar, Franklin had already been in the Arctic as captain of one of two vessels under the overall command of David Buchan which had struggled to make headway through the pack ice north of Spitsbergen in the summer of 1818. Now he was given the task of travelling up the Coppermine River to the northern coast of Canada and charting the new territory he discovered. From the beginning, his expedition was a monument to bad planning and it ended in disaster. Franklin was given only a handful of English companions for his journey. (They included George Back and John Richardson, both of whom would have roles to play in more successful expeditions in the future.) The idea was that he would recruit men from the ranks of the *voyageurs* who worked for the big Canadian trading companies. With a motley collection of followers, Franklin headed off into the wilderness, unprepared, in the summer of 1821 and almost immediately hit difficulties. Food supplies had not been properly organised and the assumption that hunting for game en route would keep them well fed soon proved nonsensical. The party was starving even before it reached the Arctic coast and matters only got worse as they undertook a dismal retreat to civilisation. They were forced to subsist on little more than handfuls of lichen which they called *tripes de roche*. Indeed, on some occasions, even that failed them. As Franklin later noted laconically in his account of the expedition, 'There was no *tripes de roche* so we drank tea and ate some of our shoes for supper'. Meanwhile the *voyageurs*, when they had the strength, regularly threatened mutiny and Richardson shot one of their number whom he suspected (probably correctly) of cannibalism. Before the party eventually reached safety, with eleven out of its twenty men dead, the survivors had endured terrible sufferings which were largely the fault of the poorness of the original planning or the ineptness of its leader's decisions at times of crisis. None of this mattered when Franklin returned home. In newspapers and the popular mind, he was now identified as 'The Man Who Ate His Boots' and he was a hero. He was not finished with the Arctic nor was it finished with him.

One of the many failed objectives of Franklin's catastrophic expedition was to rendezvous with the ships which the Admiralty had simultaneously despatched northwards under the command of William Parry, probably the most successful of Britain's Arctic explorers in this pre-Victorian era. Born in Bath in 1790, Parry had joined the Navy at the age of thirteen and gained his first experience of Arctic waters when he captained the *Alexander* in John Ross's 1818 expedition. Like most of the naval explorers under Barrow's patronage, he was not particularly enthralled by the Arctic. 'Hot or cold was all one to him,' he wrote later, referring to himself in the third person, 'Africa or the Pole.' He simply wanted the opportunities for advancement offered by the expeditions Barrow was promoting. The following year he was sent north for a second time with two ships, HMS *Hecla* and HMS *Griper*, and clear instructions to do what Ross had failed to do. He was to make his way through Lancaster Sound and journey west as far as he could. The hope, indeed almost the assumption, at the Admiralty was that he would thus find a passage to the Pacific, probably meeting up with Franklin's expedition en route. Although he did not come close to finding the elusive Northwest Passage, Parry did indeed do better than Ross. He proved that the impassable mountains the older explorer had supposedly seen were nothing of the kind and he sailed some considerable distance further west than the earlier expedition had done. However, his route was eventually blocked by ice and he and his men settled down to spend the winter on the south shore of Melville Island, an island he had just discovered and named after Viscount Melville, First Lord of the Admiralty. They were there for the best part of the next ten months, the ships frozen into the ice. When the men did manage to free the ships at the very end of July 1820, Parry was all for further attempts to sail westwards but it soon became clear that to do so was to risk being trapped in the ice's embrace for another year. He turned back towards Baffin Bay and from there sailed home to Britain.

Unlike Ross two years earlier, Parry was greeted with praise and acclamation. He may not have found the Passage but he had sailed further west in the Arctic than anyone else had done (winning a £5,000 prize offered by Parliament in the process) and he had successfully brought his party through an ice-bound winter with the loss of only one man, the victim of a previously existing lung complaint. He was the man of the moment and it was inevitable that he would be sent north again. He did not have long to wait. In April 1821, Parry set sail on his second Arctic expedition as commander. With two ships, HMS *Fury* and HMS *Hecla* (making another trip into the ice), he was again looking for a Northwest Passage but this time he was hoping to find it north of Hudson's Bay in Repulse Bay, visited and named by the navigator Christopher Middleton in the middle of the previous century. When this proved a dead end, Parry followed the coastline to the north-east, probing for an outlet or channel that would lead him back in the right direction – westwards. Openings were found but they led nowhere and, with the weather closing in, the men were driven to set up winter camp on an uninhabited island which they unimaginatively named Winter Island. As always on his expeditions, Parry worked hard to keep his men fully occupied through the long, dark and potentially soul-destroying winter months. Not only were their shipboard tasks carefully organised and planned but a theatre was established and Parry himself took one of the leading roles in an Arctic production of Sheridan's *The Rivals*.

When the sun returned and progress was again possible, the ships nudged ever further northwards, still looking for that opening to the west which, according to the Inuit with whom they had come into contact, definitely existed. They found a strait just south of Baffin Island which Parry named after his ships and which did indeed lead westwards. Unfortunately, it was completely ice-filled and impassable. Another winter beckoned and the ships retreated to the south to take shelter in a harbour they had visited earlier in the year. There were no stage shows this time but the men of the expedition fraternised extensively with the Inuit whom they seemed to view with a strange mixture of fascination and revulsion. 'These people may justly lay equal claim with ourselves to those common feelings of our nature,' Parry wrote, with more than a hint of surprise that this should be so, but he was appalled by their eating habits and by what he saw as their loose morals. It was not until July 1823 that the ice around the harbour melted sufficiently to free the ships. By this time, some of his men were suffering from scurvy and Parry was wondering whether or not another season's exploring was possible. When he visited Fury and Hecla Strait and saw that it was still frozen, he decided it was time to return to Britain. By the end of October, he was home, having been away for just over two years.

The captain of the *Hecla* on this second expedition led by Parry was George Francis Lyon, a favourite of John Barrow, who had previously attempted to make his mark in a journey to Timbuktu in Africa. That had been a disaster. Now, with Barrow's support, Lyon was given command in 1824 of the ominously named HMS *Griper* and sent out on his very own Arctic expedition. His aim was to sail into Hudson Bay and north to Repulse Bay again where he might be able to winter and then undertake an overland journey westwards. Everything went badly from the beginning. The *Griper* was a notoriously poor ship and caused endless problems. The weather that year was particularly bad and the ice in Hudson Bay was thicker and more widespread than expected. Buffeted by storms, Lyon could not carry out his plans. There even came a moment when he had to gather his crew together and advise them to prepare to meet their Maker 'as men resigned to their fate' but they somehow survived to limp back home to England with very little achieved. It was scarcely Lyon's fault but none the less he found himself no longer one of Barrow's favourites. He was never given any further opportunity to shine and he died eight years later, still only in his thirties.

At much the same time as his former subordinate was contemplating meeting his Maker in Hudson Bay, William Parry was suffering his own setbacks elsewhere in the Arctic. He had taken command of a third expedition, consisting of the two ships, HMS *Fury* and HMS *Hecla*, which sailed in May 1824. It headed for Prince Regent's Inlet which was at the west end of

Baffin Island and in a region he had visited in 1819–20. Hope springing eternal in his breast, Parry had now decided that here lay the best means of achieving the Northwest Passage. 'There is no *known* opening which seems to present itself so favourably for this purpose as Prince Regent's Inlet,' he wrote. Unfortunately he had chosen to visit the area at a time when the weather was much worse and the ice much thicker than they had been on his earlier journey. After reaching Prince Regent's Inlet and wintering there, Parry swiftly found further progress with his two ships more or less impossible. Indeed the *Fury* was driven against the shore by an iceberg and so badly damaged that she had eventually to be abandoned. The expedition limped home and Parry found his reputation as a bold explorer at its lowest ebb. Even John Barrow, who was usually his greatest supporter, was disappointed. The search for a Northwest Passage was, he wrote, 'precisely where it was at the conclusion of his first voyage'. The stage was clear for somebody else to set foot on it.

Franklin, Parry and Ross All Return to the Ice

One man who had every possible reason to avoid further Arctic travelling, it might be thought, was John Franklin but, in 1825, 'the man who ate his boots' set off on another expedition into the wilderness. With George Back and John Richardson again under his command, he aimed to follow Canada's Mackenzie River to its mouth on the Arctic Ocean. After successfully reaching its goal, the party split into two. Franklin and Back headed west while Richardson made his way east. When they all reunited in the autumn of 1826, they had, between them, travelled thousands of miles and mapped more than 1500 miles of hitherto uncharted coastline. Although they did not know it until later, Franklin's group had come within 150 miles of meeting up with a boat from another expedition under the command of Frederick Beechey which had entered Arctic waters from the Bering Strait. The man whose previous journey had been such a catastrophe had very nearly been able to show that it was possible to enter the Arctic wilderness in the east and emerge in the west.

That same year, William Parry was looking to win back some of the glory he had mislaid when his expedition to Prince Regent's Inlet had proved so unsuccessful. He was busy formulating plans to reach the North Pole and the following May he arrived in Spitsbergen to put them into action. 'Few enterprises are so easily practicable,' he wrote with admirable optimism. Unfortunately, the improbable method of transport he had chosen to try for the pole was a combination of boats and reindeer. As might perhaps have been predicted, the idea failed to work and Parry's men were reduced to dragging the boats over the ice and snow themselves. It was back-breaking toil and it was soon clear that hopes of reaching the pole had been ludicrously optimistic. As they floundered onwards, hauling the ship's boats behind them, the men were suffering badly from hunger, exhaustion and snow-blindness. By 20 July, when Parry realised that the ice over which they were making their slow progress northwards was hindering them by drifting southwards as they went, it was obvious that they had to turn back. On 26 July, they reached 82° 45' N and then joined the ice floes in heading south. The scheme for reaching the pole had been ill-conceived and could have ended in tragedy but Parry had gone further north than anyone had done before. The record was to stand for nearly fifty years. The debacle might have ruined his reputation even further but somehow it emerged not only intact but, in some ways, enhanced. The public still seemed to think highly of him.

As Parry gathered renewed plaudits, John Ross was itching to return to the Arctic and redeem *his* reputation after the dispute over what he had or had not seen in Lancaster Sound ten years earlier. Unfortunately, John Barrow was so antagonistic towards Ross that there was no chance any expedition led by him would gain Admiralty approval. Ross went in search of a private sponsor and found him in Felix Booth, a man made wealthy through the sale of Booth's Gin. In May 1829, he left England with a handful of officers and a small crew on a ship with the auspicious name of *Victory*. (The *Victory* was equipped with the novelty of a steam engine, although the engine proved almost wholly unreliable and was eventually dumped.) By August, Ross and his men had sailed beyond the point where he had turned so controversially for home in 1818 and were making new discoveries which scattered the name of their sponsor across the Arctic landscape. The Gulf of Boothia and Boothia Felix (now Boothia Peninsula) were placed on their maps and in a harbour on the latter they prepared to overwinter.

James Clark Ross, nephew of John Ross, had sailed on all three of Parry's Arctic expeditions just as he had done on his uncle's prematurely aborted mission of 1818. His relationship with his uncle had become a tempestuous one and was to grow much worse in years to come. The two men had disagreed strongly and publicly on the existence or otherwise of the mountain range the older Ross had claimed to see in Lancaster Sound. None the less, John Ross had invited his nephew to accompany him as second in command. The younger Ross now became the most active member of the expedition, undertaking a series of sledging trips from the ship to explore Boothia Felix. On one of these, he discovered and named King William Island. During another, the following year, after a second winter in the ice, he became the first man to reach the North Magnetic Pole. Distinct from the Geographic North Pole, this is the point in the northern hemisphere towards which a compass needle points. It was a remote spot in a wilderness of snow and ice, and its position had altered and would alter over time because of magnetic changes in the Earth's core, but Ross proudly raised the Union Jack and, in his own words, 'took possession of the North Magnetic Pole and its adjoining territory in the name of Great Britain and William the Fourth.'

The travels of the younger Ross were extending the list of achievements of his uncle's expedition but it began to look as if the *Victory* would never be released from the ice so that they could all go home and report them. It was August 1831 before the ice broke sufficiently for the ship to move. It travelled four miles and then was trapped again. Nothing the Rosses and their men did would free it. They had to face a third winter in the Arctic. John Ross had to consider the possibility that the ship would never get out. In the spring of 1832, he made the decision, always terrible for a captain, to abandon his ship. 'It was the first vessel that I have ever been obliged to abandon,' he later wrote sadly, 'after having served in thirty-six, during a period of forty-two years.' On 29 May 1832, he and his men left the *Victory* and made their way overland to Fury Beach where the remains of Parry's expedition of 1825 could still be found. They arrived there in July to find that some of the boats from the *Fury* were still seaworthy. Hopes of an escape rose but were dashed by the ice and the weather. The *Fury*'s boats were launched but, like the *Victory* the previous year, were unable to travel more than a few miles. Ross's expedition was doomed to a fourth winter in the ice. It was only in August 1833, by which time the men were suffering badly from scurvy, frostbite and the effects of poor food, that the boats were finally freed and could make it into open water. When Ross was finally rescued by whaling ships, the rescuers refused to believe at first that he was who he claimed to be. He couldn't be Ross, he was told, because Ross was dead. The explorer was able to tell the whalers that they had been misinformed.

The whalers had reason enough to think that Ross and his men had perished. Plenty of other people back in England were of a similar opinion. If they had not died, it was argued, they were in dire need of help. With money raised partly by the Admiralty and partly by George Ross, brother to one of the missing men and father to another, George Back was despatched on an overland mission to find out what had happened to them. He was to journey to the more remote trading posts used by the fur companies and then head north to the region in which it was assumed that the missing expedition would be. By the time Back led his party into the wilderness in the spring of 1834, he knew that Ross and his men were safe. He could concentrate on exploration of the Great Fish River (now often known by his name) which flows into the Arctic Ocean and on attempts to chart the unknown coastline around its mouth. After success in negotiating the length of the river, reaching the ocean and sighting King William Island, he decided that discretion was the better part of valour and turned back. He was home in England in September 1835.

Promoted and praised for his efforts, Back was now in Barrow's and the Admiralty's good books. He was sent out on a second expedition to try to do what Lyon had failed to achieve a decade earlier – reach Repulse Bay at the very northern end of Hudson Bay and, from there, travel overland towards the river he had investigated two years before. There was now the added hope that he might discover more about Ross's Boothia Felix. Back's journey was, if anything, even more unsuccessful than Lyon's. As he sailed through Frozen Strait towards his first destination, his ship, HMS *Terror*, was caught by the ice and remained so for the next ten months. The *Terror* was frequently under threat of destruction and, at one point, was thrust 40 feet up a cliff by the relentless force of the surrounding ice. Somehow it survived and, once the ship was finally released from the ice's embrace, Back wasted no time in heading for home. He had had enough of the Arctic and never returned there.

The fur companies had been largely indifferent to the aims of the explorers, although they had provided (sometimes grudgingly) assistance to many of the expeditions despatched into the Canadian Arctic. Their prime interest was profit not the enlargement of geographical knowledge. Now, however, the Hudson's Bay Company sponsored its own expedition to map the coastline, filling in gaps left by Franklin and others. The expedition was under the nominal leadership of Peter Dease, a long-serving employee of the company who had won the trust of Franklin during the Englishman's travels in the wilderness. However, its most forceful and flamboyant member was Thomas Simpson, Dease's second in command, who gave himself most of the credit for the expedition's successes in the years 1836 to 1839. Simpson had announced plans for further explorations but these were brought to an abrupt end when he died under mysterious circumstances while travelling across Canada with the intention of taking a ship bound for London. Officially, Simpson was said to have murdered two of his companions and committed suicide. It seems an unlikely end for such an ambitious and self-confident man. Suspicions linger that he was himself a murder victim.

Franklin and the Search for his Expedition

By 1845, the mapping out of a Northwest Passage had very nearly been achieved. Thanks to the efforts of a platoon of explorers, there were only a few hundred miles of uncharted seas between the furthest east and the furthest west that ships had travelled in the Arctic. To John Barrow, now an octogenarian, it was essential that the final connection be made and be made by a British expedition. 'If the completion of the passage be left to be performed by some other power,' he wrote, 'England, by her neglect of it... would be laughed at by all the world.' It was time for one further expedition to forge the last link in the chain. Its leader would be Sir John Franklin. Franklin was now in his late fifties. The years since his last Arctic expedition had not been particularly successful ones for him. His period as Lieutenant Governor of Van Diemen's Land (now Tasmania) had been controversial and had ended in what was (essentially) the sack. He was eager for redemption and his ambitious second wife Jane even more so.

He was not the first choice for commander of the new expedition. Barrow had approached Parry and James Ross but both had had enough of the Arctic. George Back was *persona non grata* at the Admiralty because of his difficult temperament. There were no other alternatives. Franklin it had to be. As his supporting officers he would have James Fitzjames, a protégé of Barrow in his thirties with no previous experience of polar travel, and Francis Crozier, who had served on Arctic expeditions with Parry as a young man and who had been James Clark Ross's second in command during his long Antarctic voyage. The two ships under Franklin's command, HMS *Erebus* and HMS *Terror*, had also seen service on Ross's Antarctic expedition and were considered able to deal with any possible conditions in the Arctic. When they sailed from England in May 1845, it was generally agreed by the Admiralty, the press and the public alike that the expedition was as well-equipped as any that had ever travelled northwards. Success in finally completing the Northwest Passage would surely be its reward. There were few dissenting voices, although Dr Richard King, an eccentric veteran of an expedition in the 1830s, made the memorable prediction that Franklin and his men were being sent to the Arctic to 'form the nucleus of an iceberg'. In a sense, King was right. After 26 July 1845, when two whaling ships came across *Erebus* and *Terror* in Baffin Bay, neither Franklin nor any of the 129 men with him were ever seen alive again.

For some time, the fact that there was no word from Franklin did not greatly trouble the naval authorities. It had been expected that he would be away for some time and that there would be long periods when he was out of contact with civilisation. John Ross, who had already expressed concerns about Franklin's fitness for command, offered to lead a private expedition to look for his old friend. His offer was roundly rejected. Only in 1848, three years after the expedition's departure, did the Admiralty decide that something was probably amiss and needed investigating. As if to compensate for previous inaction, three separate expeditions were now despatched to discover what they could about the lost ships and their crews. James Clark Ross made his final journey to the Arctic in charge of two ships, HMS *Investigator* and HMS *Enterprise*, but it became an ignominious failure with which to end his distinguished polar career. Another mission by sea, approaching from the Bering Strait, was led by Henry Kellett. It succeeded in charting some hitherto unmapped islands and coastline but failed to discover any signs of the missing men. John Richardson, who had travelled with Franklin on the disastrous expedition of 1819–22, was now in his sixties but he chose to join forces with a Scottish doctor named John Rae, who had worked for many years with the Hudson's Bay Company and was an experienced Arctic traveller. The two men headed overland for the wilderness regions where Franklin and his men might have been stranded. They could find no trace of them.

Within a couple of years, the Arctic was, in the words of the historian Fergus Fleming, 'crawling with rescue missions'. The major difficulty that they all had was that, given the nature of his original orders, they could not be sure what route Franklin had taken. In addition, they could not be certain that seas that were open in the years he had entered them would necessarily be still open a few years later. Factor in the sheer size of the Arctic wilderness and it becomes clear that the rescuers were looking for a tiny needle in a vast and frozen haystack.

They were, however, converging on this huge expanse of land and sea and ice from all directions. Some were sailing west from Baffin Bay. In August 1850, Erasmus Ommanney, captaining one of the ships in an expedition led by Captain Horatio Austin, made the first discovery to shed any light whatsoever on what had happened to Franklin after his encounter with the whaling ships in July 1845. On Beechey Island, named after an officer on Parry's first expedition, Ommanney came across clear indications that it had been the site of Franklin's first winter encampment.

He also found the graves of three of Franklin's men who had died and been buried on the island.

Others were sailing east from the Bering Strait. Richard Collinson in HMS *Enterprise* and Robert McClure in HMS *Investigator* left England in January 1850 with instructions to sail up the Pacific coast of the Americas and into the Arctic on a joint expedition. The two ships became separated off Chile and, from that moment onwards, acted (in effect) as two independent expeditions. McClure sailed through the Bering Strait and promptly got into difficulties. Collinson followed a year later and did little better. By now, the Admiralty was in the position of sending out rescue missions to rescue the rescue missions. In 1852, Edward Belcher was despatched to look for Franklin but he was also told to find out, if he could, what had happened to Collinson and McClure from whom nothing at that time had been heard. The latter had led an expedition bedevilled by desertion, insubordination among the officers and near-starvation. McClure was forced to abandon *Investigator* in the spring of 1853 and was lucky to be rescued by a sledging party from Belcher's expedition which took him back to their ship. In effect, he and his crew became the first men to complete the Northwest Passage. McClure had done it by sailing into the Arctic Ocean via the Bering Strait, losing his ship and being rescued by another ship which had entered from the Atlantic. It was not really the stuff of which heroic tales of derring-do could be told. It was to be another half-century before anyone was finally to achieve the Passage, this time from Atlantic to Pacific, on board one ship. On board one of the ships in Belcher's small fleet, McClure was still not safe. They were all forced to spend another winter in the ice and then Belcher retreated back home. His expedition was not a success. He had failed to find Franklin; he had decided to abandon most of the ships under his command, a decision that meant he faced a court martial when he got back to Britain; and, although his men had chanced upon McClure, he had no idea what had happened to Collinson. In fact, Collinson had spent long periods of time sailing around the Arctic Ocean, just missing contact with McClure, and had then gone back the way he had come through the Bering Strait. He was safe but he too had learned little or nothing about Franklin.

It was the independently-minded John Rae who eventually found some evidence of what had happened to the men of the *Erebus* and *Terror*. The Scottish doctor had continued to make journeys into the remote regions of the Canadian Arctic where the Franklin expedition might have ended. In March 1854, he met Inuit who told him tales of a party of about 30 or 40 white men who had died of starvation several winters earlier. Other Inuit sold him silver forks and spoons which were identified as the property of officers on the two ships. Rae's mistake, when he returned to England, was to report something else that the Inuit had told him. They had said that the remains of the dead white men showed signs that the last survivors had resorted to cannibalism in a desperate bid to stay alive. Rae was overwhelmed by a tidal wave of revulsion and disbelief from public and press when he passed on this information. Charles Dickens, a man almost unhealthily obsessed by Franklin's fate, led the way. Dismissing the reports Rae had gathered from the Inuit as 'the vague babble of savages', Dickens argued that it was completely unthinkable that the lost explorers would have resorted to what he called 'the last resource'. 'The noble conduct and example of such men,' he wrote in his weekly magazine *Household Words*, 'and of their own great leader himself, under similar endurances, belies it, and outweighs by the weight of the whole universe the chatter of a gross handful of uncivilised people, with domesticity of blood and blubber.' What the Inuit had seen, according to Dickens, were probably bodies torn and mutilated by passing polar bears.

As far as the Admiralty was concerned, the sorry saga of the Franklin expedition was over. Its members were clearly all dead and they had been officially declared as such even before John Rae arrived in Britain with his unsavoury stories of starvation and cannibalism. Lady Jane Franklin, however, was now even more determined to learn exactly what had happened to her husband. In July 1857, Francis McClintock sailed from Aberdeen in command of an expedition the formidable widow had sponsored herself. In the Arctic, he found himself in the midst of a period of unusually bad weather which restricted his search attempts but he and his men did make a series of wide-ranging sledging trips in the next two years which did eventually find new evidence of what had happened. They met with Inuit who told stories that matched the ones Rae had heard of white men starving to death in the region. Like Rae, they were offered artefacts by the Inuit which had come from Franklin's men. On 6 May 1859, a metal cylinder was found which contained a two-part note written by members of the expedition. The first part, dated 28 May 1847, said in as many words that all was then well but the second part, dated 25 April 1848 and signed by Crozier and Fitzjames, told a very different story. It reported that Franklin had died on 11 June 1847 and that nine other officers and fifteen men had also lost their lives. The ships had been abandoned in the ice a few days earlier and the remaining men were heading for 'Back's Fish River' the following day. The Great Fish River, first explored by George Back in 1834, might possibly have taken them towards settlements run by the fur companies, although it is odd that Crozier chose not to head in a direction where rescue ships might find them. In fact, they were embarked on the long trek which would eventually lead to all their deaths. McClintock's party found further confirmation of their predecessors' tragic fate when they came across some of their possessions scattered across the icy landscape and one of the ship's boats, with two skeletons in its bow.

In total nearly twenty separate expeditions were sent out to discover what had happened to the men of the *Erebus* and the *Terror*. McClintock's party, in particular, came across enough evidence for a rough map of the Franklin expedition's travels to be drawn up and for extravagant, wish-fulfilling claims that it had found the Northwest Passage to be made. (Franklin's monument in Westminster Abbey bears the inscription, 'The beloved chief of the gallant crews who perished with him in completing the discovery of the Northwest Passage'.) In fact, it had done no such thing. With a cruel irony, Franklin's greatest contribution to exploration of the Far North may well have been his disappearance. In searching for the missing expedition, other explorers not only mapped out vast areas of the wilderness. Some of them turned their attention to a new Arctic grail – the North Pole.

More Disasters Amidst the Ice: Kane, Hall, George DeLong and the American Invasion

It was not just the British who were searching for Franklin. The Americans too had begun to get in on the act. One of the most persistent and flamboyant of the American explorers was Elisha Kent Kane, scion of an upper-crust family from Philadelphia, who served as the chief medical officer on an 1850–51 expedition which had visited the site of Franklin's last camp at much the same time as Erasmus Ommanney. After returning to the USA, Kane embarked on a series of lectures on his experiences in the North, becoming in the process a famous figure who could attract financial backing for another expedition. The shipping merchant Henry Grinnell, who had sponsored the first American expedition, was prepared to put money behind a new one led by Kane. Grinnell was one of thousands fascinated by Franklin's fate and this new expedition was ostensibly intended to track down the whereabouts of the missing Englishman and his companions, whether they were alive or, as now seemed almost certain, dead. In fact, Kane had other aims firmly in mind as well.

Like many others, including the recently deceased godfather of British Arctic exploration Sir John Barrow, he was a believer in the theory of an Open Polar Sea. Push onwards through the fearsome ice, men speculated, and you would break out into clear water. The way to the pole would be revealed and it would be across open sea. Kane paid lip service to the idea of finding out about Franklin but his real interest was in sailing as far north as he could up Smith Sound in search of the Open Polar Sea. His expedition turned out to be a catalogue of disasters. After wintering further north than anyone had previously done, his men were not in prime physical condition. Indeed, some were probably suffering from scurvy. A sledging trip in March 1854 turned into a desperate rescue mission during which the rescuers were reduced to as bad a state as those they were trying to rescue. Everybody involved, including Kane himself, suffered a kind of temporary insanity as they struggled through the ice and snow back to their ship. 'I know all my companions were frantic,' one of the men later wrote, 'for they laughed immoderately, gibbered, uttered the most frightful imprecations, mimicked the screams and groans of the invalids, howled like wild beasts, and in short exhibited a scene of insane fury which I have never seen equalled in a lunatic asylum.' Back on board, the surgeon was forced to amputate toes and even, in the case of one man, an entire foot ruined by frostbite. Several of Kane's men died. The troubles of the survivors had only just begun.

Further sledging expeditions led to more suffering. The expedition was now plagued by dissension and desertion as Kane's leadership qualities were severely questioned. As it became increasingly clear that the expedition faced another winter in the Arctic, this time with inadequate provisions, Kane set off with several companions in the direction of Beechey Island, hoping to meet up with men from Belcher's expedition and beg supplies from them, but he was soon forced to return. Winter now approached and Kane's men were so divided amongst themselves that they split into two groups. One group opted to stay on the ship, the *Advance*, with Kane; the other chose to leave in the hope of reaching safety at the small Greenland settlement of Upernavik. Under the leadership of Isaac Israel Hayes, the ship's surgeon, the latter party set off at the end of August but were soon in difficulties. Unable to make it as far as the nearest outposts of civilisation and forced to build a makeshift hut to shelter them from the worsening winter weather, Hayes and the men with him eventually decided to cut their losses and return to the *Advance*. Unsurprisingly, their journey turned out to be a nightmare and, by the time they set foot on board the ship again in early December, they were lucky still to be alive.

Together with the companions they had rejoined, they still had to wait for the winter ice to melt sufficiently to allow the *Advance* to reach open water. Although the two groups had come together again, they were anything but united. Squabbling and paranoia poisoned the atmosphere on board the ship. One man deserted and made it to an Inuit village but was brought back by Kane at gunpoint. By May 1855, it was obvious both that the *Advance* was not going to be freed from the ice in the near future and that the men could not possibly survive another winter in the Arctic. The only hope for Kane's men was to abandon the ship and, dragging its smaller boats behind them, make for open water to the south. It took them a month to do so and then they were embarked on an epic journey towards settlements further south. They eventually reached safety in August. The expedition had been a nightmare but its leader drew some consolation from all the troubles. Kane was convinced that two of his men, travelling on one of the poorly planned sledging trips in the spring of 1854, had glimpsed the Open Polar Sea in which he had always believed. A few years later another expedition, led by Isaac Israel Hayes, who was returning to the Arctic despite the horrors he had experienced there, also sailed up Smith Sound and seemed to confirm its existence.

By that time Kane was dead. He passed away in 1857, still only in his late thirties, but his adventures had inspired others. His books had been bestsellers and his lecture tours sell-out successes. He had become a famous man and a catalyst for a new-found interest in the Arctic among many of his countrymen.

One of the many armchair travellers who read Kane's published journals was Charles Francis Hall. While most of Kane's readers contented themselves with merely dreaming of emulating his exploits, Hall became obsessed with the Arctic and convinced that he was destined for greatness there. He was not an experienced explorer nor was he, like so many others who had ventured into the Arctic, a naval officer. He was a pious, God-fearing printer and newspaper owner from Cincinnati and, when he set sail from New Bedford, Massachusetts in 1860 on his first Arctic expedition, it was also the first time he had ever been to sea. On his arrival in Greenland, however, he was ecstatic. 'Thank God I am at last on Arctic land where I have so long wished to be,' he wrote. 'Greenland's mountains I greet you!' After charting hundreds of miles of coastline and picking up information from the Inuit not only (he believed) on Franklin's expedition but also on Martin Frobisher's visit nearly three centuries earlier, Hall returned home delighted by his experiences and determined to return to the Arctic again.

No sooner was he back in the USA than he was planning a second expedition but, with the country plunged into civil war, it was almost impossible to raise funds for it. It was not until 1864 that Hall was able to scrape together enough cash to head for the Arctic again. This time he was to spend nearly five years away, first heading towards Repulse Bay and then travelling to King William Island, an island first explored by John Ross in 1830 which (although Hall did not know it) had been the scene of some of the worst suffering for Franklin's men two decades earlier. Hall gathered further oral testimony from the Inuit about the fate of the *Erebus* and *Terror* expedition but he was also beginning to dream of something more than just following in the footsteps of other explorers. 'Give me the means,' he wrote, 'and I will not only discover the North Pole, but survey all the land I might find between Kane's farthest and it, and have my whole soul in the work.'

In many ways, Hall was an open-minded explorer. His attitude to the Inuit (he was just about the only explorer of his times to give them the name they called themselves) was often enlightened and intelligent. Calling them 'a kind-hearted, hospitable and well-disposed race of beings', he was more prepared than most of his contemporaries to acknowledge that Western explorers had something to learn from the indigenous peoples. However, he was also muddle-headed, occasionally cantankerous and a poor leader of men. All these faults were to emerge, with disastrous consequences, in his third expedition.

By the time he embarked on it, Hall could be considered an extremely experienced polar explorer and he was able to persuade the US government to sponsor him. With his ship, the *Polaris*, he set sail from New York in June 1871 and his main aim was to make the first concerted effort to reach the North Pole since William Parry had dreamed of travelling there by reindeer power in 1827. Unfortunately, Hall's last expedition proved fatal for him and was filled with dangers for the men under his command. By the time the *Polaris* reached Greenland, dissent and insubordination, bordering on outright mutiny, were causing problems. Hall had fallen out with the scientists he had brought with him and the ship's boilers had been subjected to sabotage. As it sailed northwards, further disputes arose between Hall and his officers about just how far the ship should be taken. (It eventually reached 82° 29', the farthest north achieved for a ship up to that date.) In early September, the expedition set up its winter camp in a harbour on the northern coast of Greenland but the troubles had only just begun. Hall fell seriously ill and, on 8 November, he died. His sickness and death were (and remain) slightly mysterious. There have even been suggestions that he was murdered. Nearly a hundred years later, his body was disinterred and discovered to contain significant traces of arsenic. However, whatever the reasons for his death, it plunged the expedition into further trouble, not helped by the heavy drinking and incipient paranoia of several of those officers now left to carry out its main mission. Seven months after Hall had been buried, a small party was sent out towards the pole but it was recalled almost as soon as it had left. The *Polaris* turned southwards but was caught in the ice. One night in October, as it seemed to be threatened with destruction, a half-hearted attempt to abandon the ship ended in some of the expedition members stranded on a large ice floe. The *Polaris*, with just over a dozen men still aboard, disappeared into the night. After enduring another winter in the ice, they were rescued the following July. Meanwhile their former companions, with few supplies and limited opportunities to hunt for seal, drifted on the ice which became their home for the next six months. After suffering extremes of hunger, cold and fear, they were eventually rescued by a sealing ship in April 1873.

With the Admiralty in London still licking the wounds inflicted on its reputation by the Franklin expedition and no longer interested in the Far North, the Arctic was in danger of becoming exclusively a territory in which Americans endured, suffered and enjoyed the occasional moment of triumph. However, the late 1860s saw two minor and mostly unsuccessful expeditions despatched from north Germany under the leadership of a naval captain named Carl Koldewey. And in 1872, a new nation unexpectedly (and rather improbably) entered the annals of polar exploration. The Austro-Hungarian North Pole expedition was the brainchild of Julius von Payer, a military officer who had travelled on Koldewey's second voyage, and Karl Weyprecht, a navy lieutenant with a long-standing interest in the Arctic. Payer and Weyprecht sailed from Norway and, within a month, their ship was firmly stuck in the pack ice. Drifting at the whims of the Arctic weather, they discovered new territory, a desolate archipelago which they named after the Austro-Hungarian emperor, Franz Josef, before being forced to abandon ship and make a desperate bid to escape the ice by sledge and boat. They succeeded in reaching the Russian mainland and returning home to tell their story.

At last, after nearly twenty years of pretending that the Arctic was no longer of interest to them, the British were now stirred into action. In September 1875, a Royal Navy expedition under the command of Captain George Nares set sail from Portsmouth. Taking his ships, HMS *Alert* and HMS *Discovery* (not to be confused with the ship on Scott's first Antarctic expedition) through Smith Sound and northwards into the strait that now bears his name, Nares spent one winter amidst the ice but decided against a second and sailed home in the summer of 1876. The most notable achievement of the expedition was a sledging trip led not by Nares himself but by Albert Markham, whose cousin Clements was later to be Captain Scott's mentor and an influential advocate of Antarctic exploration as President of the Royal Geographical Society. Markham's ultimate aim when he set off in the spring of 1876 was the pole itself but it soon became clear that this would not be attainable. To his surprise, since he thought all necessary precautions had been taken to prevent it, his men began to fall sick with scurvy. By the beginning of May 1876, significant numbers of them were barely able to walk let alone haul the sledges. On 12 May, when they reached the latitude of 83° 20', Markham planted a Union Jack in the ice and they turned back towards the ship. Just over a month later they were once again on board the *Alert* but, of the fifteen-man team, one had died and only three could walk on to the ship. The others had to be carried on to it. They had reached the farthest north any human being had ever stood but they had paid a heavy price in getting there.

Despite the tragedies associated with the names of Kane and Hall, there were still plenty of Americans clamouring to win their reputations in the Far North. The most notable of these was a US naval officer called George Washington DeLong. Unfortunately, all he would succeed in doing was to add his own name to the growing list of men who had lost their lives in pursuit of Arctic dreams. With the backing of the New York newspaper proprietor James Gordon Bennett Jr, who had earlier despatched HM Stanley to Africa in search of the missing Dr

Livingstone, DeLong set sail from San Francisco on 8 July 1879. His ultimate aim was to reach the North Pole via the Bering Strait. Sadly his ship, the USS *Jeannette*, once it had reached the Arctic, rapidly became stuck in the pack ice. The *Jeannette*, with DeLong and his men on board, drifted north-west for nearly two years until, crushed by the ice, it began to break up. The explorers were forced to haul three smaller boats across the ice to open water and launch them in the direction of the Siberian mainland. One boat, with Lieutenant Charles Chipp and seven other men aboard, was never seen again. Another, commanded by the Chief Engineer George Melville, made it to the delta of the River Lena and those on it were eventually rescued and returned to the US. The fate of DeLong himself and those with him was not discovered until more than a year later when Melville, showing conspicuous bravery, returned to the region where he had nearly lost his life. He found the bodies of DeLong and his men in a snow-covered campsite close to the banks of the Lena. They had all died of cold and starvation.

By the 1880s, explorers and scientists worldwide were beginning to realise that international co-operation was required to push forward the boundaries of knowledge in the polar regions. The German scientist Georg von Neumayer and Austrian Karl Weyprecht, one of the leaders of the Austro-Hungarian expedition of 1872–74, were in the forefront of the campaign to co-ordinate activities. Weyprecht died in 1881 but their work reached fruition that same year with the institution of the First International Polar Year. Twelve nations, including Britain, the USA, Norway and Russia, signed up to participate and fifteen expeditions were organised, most of them in the Arctic, to establish research stations. It was the beginning of modern scientific investigation of the polar regions but the International Polar Year (which, confusingly, is often described as lasting from 1881 to 1884) was marked by tragedy. The American contribution to the international efforts, sometimes known as the Lady Franklin Bay expedition, was led by Adolphus

Greely, an army officer who had no previous experience in the Arctic but had served with bravery and distinction as a young man in the Civil War. Greely set up camp well north of the Arctic Circle at a site he called Fort Conger. A small sledging party led by one of his officers, James B Lockwood, achieved a farthest north of 83° 24', beating Markham's record by a scant few miles, but the expedition was otherwise disastrous. Attempts to supply Fort Conger failed miserably and Greely abandoned it in August 1883. He headed south to a place where he believed ships would have deposited food and fuel. They hadn't and Greely's men were forced to spend the winter there in terrible circumstances. By the time rescuers did reach them in 1884, nineteen of his twenty-five men had died (one of them had been shot by Greely for mutiny) and the survivors had had to resort to cannibalising the corpses of their dead colleagues in order to stay alive.

Farthest North: Nansen and the Fram

Meanwhile in the Russian Arctic, some long-cherished goals were finally being achieved. Unlike the Northwest Passage, which might have simply been a geographical chimera, the Northeast Passage undoubtedly existed. By the middle of the nineteenth century, there could be no argument that it was possible to sail across the top of Russia from the Atlantic to the Pacific. It was just that it was extraordinarily difficult and nobody had done it. This was about to change. Adolf Erik Nordenskjöld was a Finnish-Swedish nobleman, exiled from the Grand Duchy of Finland (then under Russian rule) for his political activities, who had taken part in a series of small-scale Arctic expeditions in the 1860s and early 1870s. In the summer of 1878, he set sail in his ship the *Vega* and passed Cape Chelyuskin, the northernmost point of the Russian mainland, in August. The following month, the *Vega* was frozen into the ice near the Bering Strait. Concerns grew back in Europe that the expedition might be in trouble. (Ironically, one of the subsidiary objectives of George DeLong was to offer assistance to Nordenskjöld. As it turned out, DeLong was far more in need of help than the man he was thinking he might have to rescue.) However, Nordenskjöld and his men simply waited out the long Arctic winter and then navigated their way to Port Clarence in Alaska in July 1879.

With the Northeast Passage completed, it remained for someone to make an equivalent journey in the Canadian Arctic or travel successfully to the pole. It was now time for one of the greatest and most widely gifted of all Arctic explorers to step on to the stage. Fridtjof Nansen was originally a scientist. If he had never chosen to travel north, he might still be remembered, if not so widely, for his research into the central nervous system. He was born on a country estate north of Oslo, then known as Christiania, in 1861 and grew up as a great enthusiast for the Norwegian national sports of skiing and skating. At the same time that he was studying zoology at the Royal Frederick University in Christiania, he was also making his mark as a winter sportsman. He held world records in distance skating and became national cross-country skiing champion for the first of eleven times in 1880. However, as he continued his academic work and his sporting activities, his mind was turning towards Arctic exploration and discovery. In 1888, together with a party which included Otto Sverdrup, destined to become a close colleague and the leader of several expeditions of his own in the Arctic, Nansen made the first crossing of Greenland from east to west.

This was a substantial achievement in itself but the Norwegian adventurer now had more ambitious plans in mind. He had devised a daring and original method of travel which he believed would enable him to reach the North Pole. He would use the natural drift of the ice floes to take him there. A ship, suitably strengthened against the ice, would enter the pack in the seas off Siberia. It would be trapped and the ocean current beneath, flowing from east to west, would take it towards Greenland via the pole. Soon, Nansen had his ship which he called the *Fram*, Norwegian for 'Forward'. He had his crew which included Otto Sverdrup as his second in command. In July 1893, he set out from Norway towards Novaya Zemlya and then aimed to follow the Siberian coastline eastwards until he could pick up the drift west and (most importantly) north which he hoped would get him to the pole. Unfortunately, it didn't. Progress was painfully slow and by November 1894 it was clear that Nansen's original plan was not going to work. He announced another one to his crew but a further four months were to pass before this could be put into action. Finally, in March 1895, together with one companion named Hjalmar Johansen, he left the ship and set off for the pole with sledges, dogs and skis.

They made good progress at first but soon the natural phenomenon which Nansen had originally hoped would work in his favour on board the *Fram* began to work against them. The ice was beginning to drift southwards as they struggled to make their way northwards. In effect, for every two steps they took forward, the moving pack ice ensured that they also took one back. At this rate, Nansen's calculations suggested that they would not have enough food to get to the pole and back. They would have to retreat. The final camp before the two men turned southwards was at 86° 13'. They had travelled nearly three degrees of latitude further north than the sledging party in Greely's ill-fated expedition but it was no good. The North Pole remained unattainable. Once they were heading away from the pole, new difficulties arose. Their chronometers, needed for working out longitude and the direction in which safety lay, both stopped working. The ice was becoming slushier and making travel more difficult. In August 1895, they reached land which they assumed was Franz Josef Land but, without the essentials for navigation, they could not be sure. The weather was becoming bad and they were soon forced to set up a winter camp. They were able to hunt and food was no longer a problem but they had to endure months of waiting before they could resume their trek back to civilisation. In May 1896, they left their winter camp and started their journey again. On 17 June, the two men were hunched over their meagre morning meal when Nansen claimed that he could hear dogs barking. Johansen said it was impossible but his leader insisted. He set off to investigate and some time later spotted the figure of a man against the snow. The figure approached, looked him up and down and said, 'Aren't you Nansen?' The man was Frederick Jackson, an English explorer who was mapping the many uncharted areas of Franz Josef Land. It was an extraordinarily fortuitous meeting but, without it, Nansen and Johansen might well have died and news of their extraordinary attempt on the pole would never have reached the outside world.

On his return to Norway, Nansen decided that he had had enough of exploration. He devoted his genius to other activities and was a leading figure in the campaign and negotiations which led to Norway separating from Sweden and once again emerging as an independent, sovereign state. In the aftermath of the First World War, he became the League of Nations' High Commissioner for Refugees and he was awarded the 1922 Nobel Peace Prize for his work. Nansen himself may not have ventured into the high North again but his innovations in polar travel, his epic journey with Johansen and his example continued to be enormously influential on future generations of explorers both in the Arctic and the Antarctic.

Swedes and Italians: Salomon Andrée and the Duke of Abruzzi

There were other men who advocated new methods of travelling across the Arctic landscape, although not always with the knowledge and insight of Nansen. One of these men was Salomon Andrée, a Swedish engineer who worked for his country's patent office. Andrée was an enthusiast for ballooning and he saw no reason why balloonists might not travel to the North Pole. He set about raising funds for a voyage by hydrogen balloon which would, he hoped, take him from the Svalbard archipelago across the top of the world. The idea was greeted eagerly in Sweden. Support came from national scientific bodies and financial aid from prominent Swedes such as Alfred Nobel, the inventor of dynamite. Together with Nils Strindberg, a photographer and second cousin of the playwright August Strindberg, and the engineer Knut Frænkel, Andrée set off in his balloon on 11 July 1897. The three men were not seen again for more than thirty years. Only in 1930 were their bodies found and the story of their expedition told. The primitive steering mechanism for the balloon had failed from the beginning (two out of the three ropes of which it consisted had been lost on take-off) and Andrée and his companions had been forced on to the pack ice after less than three days in the air. Hauling sledges that they had stored on the balloon, they set off for a supply depot which had already been established in case of misadventure. They never made it. They reached solid land on a small island in the north-east of the Svalbard archipelago but they were all suffering from diarrhoea and swelling of the limbs (probably caused by trichinosis, a disease they may have contracted from eating worm-infected polar bear meat) and they died within days of landing. The first attempt to reach the pole by balloon had been a disaster from start to finish.

Prince Luigi Amedeo Giuseppe Maria Ferdinando Francesco of Savoy-Aosta, Duke of the Abruzzi, was the most socially distinguished individual to venture into the region before Prince Harry made his Arctic trek in 2011. He was born in Madrid in 1873. At the time of his birth his father happened to be King of Spain (although he abdicated when his younger son was less than a month old) but the Duke was first and foremost a member of the Italian royal family. He was a grandson of Victor Emmanuel II, the first king to rule a united Italy. At the time of Abruzzi's Arctic expedition, his uncle Umberto I was the Italian king. A veteran of mountaineering expeditions in the Alps and Alaska, the Duke turned his attention to the North Pole in 1899. In a ship named the *Stella Polare*, he and his carefully chosen companions headed for the northernmost point of Franz Josef Land. The idea was to winter there and then the duke would lead a smaller party pole-wards.

Unfortunately, winter conditions were bad. Frostbite attacked many of the men, including Abruzzi. Two of the ducal fingers had to be removed. Any thoughts he may have had about leading the proposed polar journey himself had to be abandoned and command passed to his comrade, Umberto Cagni. Cagni headed northwards from Franz Josef Land on 11 March 1900 with ten men and more than a hundred dogs to haul the sledges loaded with supplies. The idea was for two support teams of three men to turn back at given points, leaving Cagni and three companions to make it as far as the pole. The plan worked insofar as the support teams headed back to the *Stella Polare* as intended (although one of them vanished without trace en route and its fate is still unknown) but trouble was soon brewing. The weather was against them and they were unable to travel the distances they needed to do in order to keep to the tight timetable they had organised. Food was also running low and it soon became clear that the pole was beyond their grasp. On 25 April, Cagni and his men reached 86° 34', the northernmost point then achieved and some twenty miles further than Nansen and Johansen had travelled in 1895. The Italians planted a flag and turned for home. At first the going was deceptively easy but within a few weeks their journey turned into a desperate race for survival. The ice was beginning to melt and it was also drifting in the very direction they did not want to go. As they marched eastwards towards the *Stella Polare* on the shore of Franz Josef Land, the ice was perversely determined to carry them westwards to their doom. It was not until the end of June, with supplies and fuel running low, that they finally managed to get back to the ship.

Roald Amundsen Finally Does It

For centuries British and American expeditions had been searching for a Northwest Passage in the hope that it would provide a new and commercially rewarding means of getting from the Atlantic to the Pacific and vice versa. Hundreds of men had lost their lives in the search. Robert McClure had made the journey from west to east in the 1850s but he had done it partly by ship, partly by sledge and partly in the company of those who had come from the east to rescue him. His journey was scarcely the stuff of which legend was made. By the end of the nineteenth century, it was clear that there were passages that could be traced through the maze of islands, inlets and straits that made up the Canadian Arctic but no one had yet traversed it in one expedition and one ship. It was left to a Norwegian to perform this last heroic deed and, as had been increasingly clear throughout most of the century, the Passage proved to have no commercial value whatsoever.

The Norwegian was Roald Amundsen. He was born in 1872 in Borge, a small village near the city of Frederikstad in south-eastern Norway. He came from a family of shipowners and sea captains but, to please his mother, he trained to become a doctor. Only when she died did he give up his medical studies and go to sea. From boyhood, Amundsen had been fascinated by tales of polar exploration (the mystery surrounding the Franklin expedition was a particular favourite) and his ambition was always to travel in the Arctic. Nansen's crossing of Greenland, which took place when Amundsen was in his teens, was another spur to achievement. However, the first major polar expedition in which he participated was one to the South rather than the North. Between 1897 and 1899, he was first mate of the *Belgica*, the ship under the captaincy of Adrien de Gerlache which was the first to spend an entire, sunless winter in the Antarctic.

On his return to Norway, Amundsen began to plan his

expedition to navigate the Northwest Passage. He consulted Nansen, already the elder statesman of Arctic exploration, and gained the benefits of both his advice and his blessing on the project. He found his ship – a 47-ton fishing vessel named the *Gjoa* – and he recruited six companions to share the rigours of the journey with him. Finances were trickier. In June 1903, with creditors threatening to take possession of his ship, he left Oslo and sailed for Baffin Bay. Taking a route through a landscape that was dominated by physical features named after the explorers who had gone before him (Parry Channel, James Ross Strait, Rae Strait), Amundsen reached King William Island in September. He sailed into a harbour that is now home to a small settlement named Gjoa Haven after his ship and stayed there for nearly two years. Only in the summer of 1905 did the *Gjoa* resume its journey. It reached Cambridge Bay where James Collinson, sailing from the Bering Strait, had wintered in 1852–53. The Northwest Passage from east to west had been completed but, with another winter approaching, Amundsen now needed to get word of his achievement to the outside world. He left his ship to winter again amidst the ice and made his way overland for 800 miles to the nearest telegraph station. From there he wired the news back to Europe. After five hundred years of trying, the Northwest Passage had finally been achieved.

The Antarctic Pre-1900

Eighteenth-Century Voyages South: Cook and others

In the middle of the eighteenth century, many people still believed in the possible existence of *Terra Australis*, the great continent which geographers since classical times had suggested must lie in southern latitudes to balance the land masses in the North. Previous centuries had seen explorers such as the Dutchman Abel Tasman go in search of this half-fabled land which was thought to be temperate in its climate, rich in its vegetation and, like the Americas, home to unknown peoples. Indeed, when Tasman reached what we now know was New Zealand in December 1642, he assumed it was part of a much larger continent which stretched across the southern seas. Just over a hundred years later, the reality or otherwise of *Terra Australis* was still a matter of debate and a number of expeditions, largely French and British, were despatched to look for it. Philip Carteret, Samuel Wallis and Louis de Bougainville all succeeded in circumnavigating the world (and the latter had a flower, the Bougainvillea, named after him) but none found any sign of a great southern continent. The Breton naval officer Yves-Joseph de Kerguelen-Trémarec sailed far enough south to discover the Kerguelen Islands, to which he lent half of his impressive surname. He believed at first that he might have stumbled upon the land for which his king, Louis XV, had instructed him to look but they turned out to be nothing more than a desolate, rocky archipelago.

However, indisputably the greatest of these explorers was the Yorkshireman James Cook. Cook's first voyage, between 1768 and 1771, had been to observe the transit of Venus, a rare but important astronomical phenomenon, from the Pacific island of Tahiti. During the course of it, he made his first landings in New Zealand and on the eastern coastline of Australia which he claimed as British territory. On his second voyage, he was given direct instructions by the Admiralty to search for *Terra Australis* and to discover whether or not lands he had seen on his previous voyage could be part of it. Cook was no great believer in the idea of the Great Southern Continent but he was determined to do as thorough a job as he could in deciding the question of its existence one way or the other. Circumnavigating the globe at high latitude, he found no trace of anything that matched the speculations of armchair geographers through the centuries. During the course of his extraordinary journey, on 17 January 1773, Cook and his companions aboard the *Resolution* and the *Discovery* became the first men known to have crossed the Antarctic Circle. They had been fighting their way through the pack ice for weeks before this and the cold was growing too intense for them to bear. The ships were clearly in danger and Cook turned northwards.

Cook finally put paid to the notion of the *Terra Australis* as geographers of the past had imagined it (although a few eccentrics persisted in clinging to the idea well into the nineteenth century) but he opened up new possibilities for future explorers. Some of these possibilities were in Australia, New Zealand and the Pacific; others were in the bleak waters which Cook had found further south. There might be no temperate continent peopled by new races of men and women but there was something down there at the bottom of the earth. 'I strongly believe that there does exist land close to the Pole,' Cook wrote in 1777, 'from which must proceed the greater part of the ice which we find spread across this vast southern ocean.' It was now up to others to locate this land.

First Sighting and First Landing:
Bellingshausen and Davis

It was to be many decades before anyone did. 1820 was the year in which the first sightings of Antarctica were made. Edward Bransfield was an Irishman, born in County Cork in 1785, who had risen through the ranks of the Royal Navy to become master of HMS *Andromache*, flagship of a naval squadron patrolling the coast of South America in the autumn of 1819. Bransfield was given the job of commanding a brig named the *Williams* and despatched southwards to survey what are now known as the South Shetland Islands, recently discovered by an English mariner named William Smith. In January of the following year, sailing beyond the South Shetlands, he and his men (who now included Smith) glimpsed Trinity Peninsula, the northernmost point of the Antarctic mainland, on the 30th of that month. What Bransfield did not, and could not, know was that two days earlier the Russian captain (later admiral) Fabian Gottlieb von Bellingshausen had sighted another part of Antarctica. Bellingshausen had a far more distinguished record as a cartographer and explorer than Bransfield. As a young man, he had taken part in the first Russian circumnavigation of the world between 1803 and 1806. When the Tsar gave his blessing to another major naval expedition in 1819, Bellingshausen was an obvious choice as its commander. Sailing from Kronstadt with two ships, he made his way to the southern ocean via Britain where he met up with the now elderly Sir Joseph Banks who had accompanied Cook on his first voyage fifty years earlier.

Bransfield was a Royal Navy officer; Bellingshausen was a Russian naval captain commissioned by his Tsar to sail south. However, most of the men in Antarctic waters in the 1820s were there primarily to hunt the wildlife. An American seal hunter named Nathaniel Palmer, commanding his first ship at the age of only twenty-one, sailed in search of seal colonies that had not yet been plundered and became the third person to sight the Antarctic mainland in November 1820.

A few months later, in February 1821, another sealer, the British-born John Davis may have become the first person actually to set foot on Antarctica. His claims have been disputed and never verified beyond all doubt. If he and his men were there, they did not linger long. This possible first landing on the Antarctic continent lasted about an hour. What is certain is that Davis, although he could not be sure that he was right, was convinced that the territory he had seen and (perhaps) visited was more than just an island. 'I think this Southern Land to be a Continent,' he wrote in his log. It was to take more than a century for the full extent of this new continent to be mapped.

Weddell, Ross and Wilkes

The early exploration of Antarctic waters continued to be largely the work of sealers and whalers who combined the desire for profit with a taste for exploration. The most successful of these men was James Weddell. Born in 1787, Weddell first went to sea at the age of only nine and, by the time he made his first voyage to Antarctica in 1819, he had already had a widely varied career in both the Royal Navy and the merchant service. Attracted south initially by the commercial prospect of finding new sealing grounds, he showed himself just as interested in exploration and charting new lands. He gave the name of the South Orkneys to a group of islands which he was amongst the first to visit and, in February 1823, on his third Antarctic voyage, he and his crew sailed their ship, the *Jane*, to 74° 34', a record furthest south. Patriotically, he named the sea he discovered in his record-setting journey after his king, George IV, but, since 1900, it has been called the Weddell Sea.

Seven years later, another merchant sailor named John Biscoe was employed by the London-based company Enderby & Sons to undertake exploratory voyages in the southern oceans in search of new whaling grounds to exploit. After visiting the

South Shetlands, Biscoe sailed further south. In the course of an extensive journey which made him only the third person (after Cook and Bellingshausen) to complete a circumnavigation of the mostly undiscovered continent, he sighted two significant stretches of new coastline which he named Enderby Land (after his employer) and Graham Land (after the First Lord of the Admiralty at the time).

In America, there were those who argued that what Biscoe had found and named as Graham Land was actually nothing more than another part of Palmer's Land, already discovered and named by the American sealer Nathaniel Palmer ten years before. Indeed supporters of Palmer's precedence also argued for the importance of the Antarctic to American interests and proposed more organised expeditions from the USA to southern waters. Their pleas largely fell on deaf ears. Meanwhile, a nobleman from Normandy named Jules Dumont D'Urville, convinced that anything English sealers and whalers could do, a French naval officer could do better, had sailed into Antarctic waters with two ships, the *Astrolabe* and the *Zélée*, intent on pushing beyond Weddell's furthest south. Dumont D'Urville already had an unusual claim to fame. In 1820, while cruising around the Greek islands, he had been largely responsible for the discovery of the Venus de Milo and its recognition as a significant piece of classical statuary. Now he was venturing south in search of greater fame. His ships reached the South Shetlands and charted other islands beyond them but the pack ice was troublesome and his men began to show signs of scurvy. In February 1838, still well short of Weddell's line of latitude, Dumont D'Urville was forced to turn back. After an eighteen-month period of rest and recuperation in the Pacific and Tasmania, he headed south again, this time hoping to reach the South Magnetic Pole. Again the Frenchman fell short of his goal. His voyage was not without its achievements, however. He had sighted a distant coastline which he named Adélie Land after his wife, and which has formed the basis for French claims in Antarctica to the present day; he had also made discoveries enough to fill a multi-volume official report on his voyage that was published some years after his return home. Sadly, Dumont D'Urville did not live very long to enjoy his expanded reputation. In 1842, a train derailed near Versailles, killing more than fifty passengers. The explorer and the wife for whom he named a stretch of icy coastline were amongst the victims of the accident.

Attempts to arouse interest in exploration in southern waters in America had finally borne fruit. The United States Exploring Expedition, led by Charles Wilkes, set off from Virginia in August 1838. Wilkes was in charge of a small fleet of ships and, in addition to the sailors to man them, he had a small platoon of scientists from mineralogists to a languages expert on board. The expedition was to last four years and to take Wilkes and the men with him thousands and thousands of miles around the globe. During the course of it, the ships twice entered Antarctic waters, in the early months of 1839 and again at much the same time in the following year. Sailing along the edge of the pack ice in the seas south of Australia for more than a thousand miles, Wilkes sighted land on several occasions. In recognition of his achievements and of the fact that these sightings effectively provided the first major proofs that Antarctica was a continent, that part of the mainland is now known as Wilkes Land.

At more or less the same time as Dumont D'Urville and Wilkes were making their discoveries, an English explorer of great experience was also venturing into the southern oceans. Indeed, few, if any, English explorers had more experience than James Clark Ross. Sailing with his uncle Sir John Ross and with Sir William Parry, he had already, as we have seen, made a name for himself in the Arctic. For two decades he had spent at least part of each year in the Arctic and had overwintered amidst the ice and snow in eight of those years. Now, in 1839, he took command of an expedition which was to write his name over the landscape of Antarctica (the Ross Sea, the Ross Ice Shelf) and confirm him as one of the greatest polar explorers of the nineteenth century. Just as he had located the North Magnetic Pole eight years earlier, he now hoped to locate its equivalent in the Antarctic. After being entertained in Hobart by his old friend John Franklin, now Lieutenant Governor of Tasmania, he crossed the Antarctic Circle with his two ships, *Erebus* and *Terror*, at the beginning of 1841 and soon sighted a mountainous coastline stretching south into the distance. He was unable to land there and was forced to content himself with naming it Victoria Land after the new queen back home.

There were other and more astonishing discoveries to make. Two volcanoes were seen, one of them 'emitting flame and smoke in great profusion'. Ross named them after his two ships. However, he had reached the limit of his travels south. A vast ice shelf, which was later to bear his name, stretched across the horizon, blocking his path. As *Erebus* and *Terror* drew closer it was clear that he could go no further. 'We might as well sail through the cliffs of Dover as penetrate such a mass,' Ross commented. Escaping from the pack ice on 8 March, Ross paused only to confirm that what his American rival Wilkes, from a distance, had thought was land was actually open sea. Then he sailed back to Tasmania and another open-armed welcome from Franklin. Ross made two further forays south in 1842 and 1843. On the first of these he was able to travel to an ever so slightly lower latitude than he had done the previous year before again being stopped by the Barrier ice and forced to retreat. After a miserable sojourn in the Falklands, his third trip beyond the Antarctic Circle proved even less successful than the second and he sailed for England. The *Erebus* and the *Terror* arrived home in September 1843, nearly four and a half years after their original departure.

Norwegians and Others: Larsen, Bull, De Gerlache and Borchgrevink

For the next fifty years interest in Antarctic regions faded. Polar explorers seeking glory seemed more likely to find it in the Far North than the Far South. Commercial ventures in search of whales and seals were easier and more profitable in northern rather than southern waters. There were few compelling reasons to travel to Antarctica and, for half a century, few did. However, as the nineteenth century drew to a close, there was renewed interest in the region. Once again Antarctica became a desirable destination for both those with commercial reasons for visiting (whalers and sealers) and those who simply wished to fill in the largest remaining blank on the map of the world. Between 1890 and 1905, the number of expeditions sailing south reached double figures. In the *Jason*, a ship once used in Greenland waters by the great Nansen himself, the Norwegian Carl Larsen made a series of territorial discoveries in 1892 and 1893. Another Norwegian, Henrik Bull, financed like Larsen by a whaling company, anchored off Cape Adare, at the northernmost point of Sir John Ross's Victoria Land in January 1895 in his ship *Antarctic*. Several of the *Antarctic*'s crew stepped ashore.

Three years later, members of an expedition led by the Belgian naval officer Adrien de Gerlache became the first men to experience the miseries of an Antarctic winter. Their ship, the *Belgica*, was caught fast in the pack ice of the Bellingshausen Sea in late February of 1898. Nearly three months later the total darkness of the winter night descended on them and lasted until the end of July. It was not until the following March, just over a year after their ordeal began, that they were finally able to break free of the ice and head north under their own steam. Among de Gerlache's men, several of whom were driven to the point of madness by their experiences, were two individuals who were to play larger roles in the future history of polar exploration, one in the north and one at both ends of the earth. The American physician Frederick Cook won the respect of his colleagues with his unrelenting efforts to preserve their health and sanity through the long, black nights; and, as we have seen, the Norwegian Roald Amundsen, then in his twenties, served as the *Belgica*'s first mate.

A few weeks before the *Belgica* broke free of the ice on 14 March 1899, another ship, the *Southern Cross*, arrived at Cape Adare on the Antarctic mainland and established a base. The party was led by Carsten Borchgrevink, the son of a Norwegian father and an English mother, who had already spent time in Antarctica as a member of Henrik Bull's earlier expedition. Indeed, he claimed that he had been the very first person to set foot on the Antarctic mainland. (There is much debate on this subject and, as we have seen, a British sealer named Davis may well have beaten him to the record by seventy years and more. There is even argument about whether or not Borchgrevink was the first man in the Bull expedition to stand on the Antarctic continent. Others on the voyage made the same claim.) Funded by the British magazine publisher Sir George Newnes, Borchgrevink was now back in the Antarctic with an expedition which included biologists, physicists and other scientists. The men overwintered at Cape Adare and, despite the morale-shattering loss of one of their colleagues, the young Norwegian zoologist Nicolai Hanson who died of a puzzling intestinal disease and achieved the dubious honour of becoming the first person to be buried on the Antarctic mainland, they carried out significant scientific work. With the winter over, the *Southern Cross* sailed further south and landed at what would later be called the Bay of Whales. With two companions, Borchgrevink succeeded in climbing on to the Great Ice Barrier, later known as the Ross Ice Shelf, and sledging a short distance southwards. He had established a new Farthest South at 78° 50'. The time had come for him to return home.

In their different ways, Adrien de Gerlache, Henrik Bull and

Carsten Borchgrevink had led successful expeditions which had achieved notable firsts in Antarctic history. However, the most significant of all expeditions to the Far South in the last few years of the nineteenth century and the first few years of the twentieth century was about to arrive in the ice and snow. This was Scott's *Discovery* Expedition but, before we consider that, we must turn our attention again to the other end of the world. The North Pole was about to be claimed but in very controversial circumstances.

First to the North Pole: Arguments and Debates

Peary and Henson

Fergus Fleming, in his book *Ninety Degrees North*, described Robert Edwin Peary as 'undoubtedly the most driven, possibly the most successful, and probably the most unpleasant man in the annals of polar exploration'. Peary was born in Pennsylvania in 1856 and moved to Maine with his mother when he was a young child, following the death of his father. He took an engineering degree at Bowdoin College, graduating in 1877, and joined the US Navy four years later. However, he was to spend very little of his career actually serving as a naval engineer. His first encounter with the Arctic came in 1886 when he landed at the small port of Godhavn on the west coast of Greenland. His intention was to travel eastwards by dog sled and cross the vast island from one side to the other, a feat nobody had previously achieved. He was not successful and had to turn back after journeying just short of 100 miles into the interior. Showing the gift for overpraising his own endeavours which was to stand him in good stead in years to come, Peary claimed that he had none the less 'gone a greater distance than any white man previously'.

In the 1890s, he returned to Greenland on three separate expeditions in 1891–2, 1893–5 and 1898–1902. Each time he nudged ever further northwards and closer to his ultimate goal of the pole. Each time he returned to America, his fame grew. On two of the expeditions he was accompanied by his wife

Josephine who thus became the first Western woman to take part in an Arctic expedition. Despite setbacks and injuries – he broke his leg on one trip and lost most of his toes to frostbite on another – he gradually increased his Arctic skills and became the most experienced polar traveller that America had so far produced. In his attitude to the Inuit, Peary was, in many ways, the epitome of the arrogant white man, patronising and paternalistic in his approach to the indigenous people he came across. In one now notorious incident in his career, he brought a small group of Inuit back to the USA to be displayed to a public eager to gawp at them. When, one by one, the Inuit sickened and died, their bodies were stripped of their flesh and their bones exhibited in the American Museum of Natural History in New York as if they were little different to the polar bears and other Arctic fauna already on display there. And yet Peary, more than almost any other Arctic explorer before him, was prepared to learn from the Inuit. It proved the basis for his success.

In July 1905, he set off from New York on yet another expedition, sailing north in a ship named *Roosevelt* after the US President and captained by Robert Bartlett, a man who was to play a significant role both in Peary's future life and the history of Arctic exploration. Under Bartlett's guidance, the *Roosevelt* nudged and battled its way through the ice in the channel between Ellesmere Island and Greenland to a winter base at Cape Sheridan. There they stayed until the weather was suitable for an attempt on the pole some 500 miles further north. In March, Peary and his sledging teams set off on the journey. For some weeks they made good progress but a number of factors (bad weather, the drift of the ice and the opening of a wide lead in it) combined to slow them down. It became clear that the pole would elude Peary again. He made a dash for a new Farthest North record. On 21 April 1906, according to Peary, he reached 87° 6'. On his return to the USA, he was acclaimed for pushing the record ever closer to the pole but there have always been those who have doubted whether he did what he claimed. They have pointed to the astonishing daily mileages clocked up. Could Peary and his companions really have travelled as far and as fast as they said they had? It was a question that was to be asked again about the final journey to the North Pole three years later.

When Peary set sail from New York on 6 July 1908, he must have known that this was probably his last chance to reach the pole. He was now in his early fifties and the Arctic was not an environment that was kind to middle-aged men. The captain of his ship, the *Roosevelt*, was once again Robert Bartlett and he steered the vessel as far north as the northern coast of Ellesmere Island, some 500 miles from the pole. There the expedition spent the winter and then, at the end of February 1909, Peary's final trek to his much longed-for goal began. Support parties turned back at various points in the journey until, on 31 March, at 87° 47' N, a last parting of the ways took place. One group would head back to base; the other would go on to the pole. Robert Bartlett was assuming that he would be in the final polar party. Peary had as good as promised that he would be. However, the *Roosevelt*'s captain was to be disappointed. He was told that he would be returning with the final support party. In an appearance before a Congressional committee two years later, Peary was blunt enough about his reasons for sending Bartlett back. 'I did not feel that I was called upon to divide my honours with any man, however able and deserving, who had put only a few years of his life into the work, and who did not have the same right to the honour of discovery which I felt I had.' In other words, he did not want anybody to share his glory.

As Bartlett turned sadly for the camp at Ellesmere Island, Peary set off to cover the last 133 miles to the pole with four Inuit hunters and a man named Matthew Henson. Why was Peary, a man who was almost pathologically angered by rivals and by those whom he considered trespassers on territory that was his, prepared to countenance any non-Inuit companion on this polar journey? If Bartlett was a problem, why was Henson not? The likeliest answer is that Matthew Henson was black. Although Peary undoubtedly admired and respected him, he could never be, in Peary's eyes, a true rival in the same way that a white man might have been. Henson was born in Maryland in 1866 and became a sailor on merchant ships when he was in his teens. He was twenty-one when he first met Peary and he had gone on to be his fellow traveller on nearly all of his earlier journeys. Now he was to share in Peary's greatest triumph. On April 6, Peary said, the six men reached the pole. It was the realisation of a dream that Peary had nurtured for half his lifetime. And yet there was a significant fly in Peary's ointment. When he returned to civilisation, he learned that another explorer was also claiming to have reached the North Pole. Even more irritatingly, he was saying that he had arrived there nearly a full year before Peary and Henson had done so. The person with the gall to make what seemed to Peary this outrageous claim was a man he knew of old – Dr Frederick Cook.

Frederick Cook and the Doubtful Claim

Born in a small town in New York State in 1865, Cook had moved with his mother to Brooklyn after his father's early death. He went on to study medicine at Columbia University and, little more than a year after receiving his MD, he joined an Arctic expedition as its surgeon and physician. The leader of the expedition was Robert Peary, the man with whom he was to engage in a furious controversy nearly twenty years later. As we have already seen, five years after returning from the Arctic, Cook headed to the opposite end of the earth and was one of those pioneers aboard de Gerlache's *Belgica* who were the first to winter in Antarctica. On both these expeditions, Cook behaved with exemplary determination and was considered a tough, intelligent and courageous companion by his peers. By the time the twentieth century dawned, he had won a reputation as one of the ablest of all living polar explorers. In 1901, when Peary was thought to be in trouble in the Arctic, it was Cook who was sent northwards with a relief ship. He was appalled by what he found and by the condition of Peary and those with him but the older explorer, never one to pay much attention to anybody's opinion but his own, dismissed his concerns. Cook provided some medical help and urged Peary to return home. Peary refused and Cook had no option but to sail away, leaving his fellow explorer to carry on as he thought best.

In 1903, Cook organised an expedition of his own, travelling to Alaska and mapping hitherto uncharted territory as he circled Mount McKinley, North America's highest mountain, looking for a means to ascend it. On this occasion, he was unsuccessful, despite making two attempts on the mountain, but he returned to Alaska in 1906 and claimed to have reached McKinley's summit. No one had reason to doubt that he had done so. Cook returned to New York to public acclaim and was elected President of the city's Explorers' Club. He was now ready to put his most ambitious plan so far into action and try for the North Pole. He travelled to a small settlement in the north of Greenland named Annoatok. He left Annoatok in the spring of 1908 and disappeared from public view for just over a year. When he re-surfaced, he had a tale to tell. According to Cook, he had been accompanied by two Inuit on a sledging journey across the frozen Smith Sound to Ellesmere Island. From there he had travelled west across that island to Axel Heiberg Island and then turned north. Again according to Cook, he had reached the pole on 22 April 1908. 'I had culminated with success the efforts of all the brave men who had failed before me,' he later wrote. Unfortunately, not everybody believed him.

In the fierce debates that followed, Peary's supporters looked back at Cook's earlier achievements and claimed that he had a track record for fraudulent assertions about what he had done. He had not, they said, succeeded in reaching the summit of Mount McKinley and they persuaded his companion on that climb, a man named Ed Barrill, to sign an affidavit denying that the peak had been conquered. (Barrill was paid a significant sum of money to affix his signature to the document which cynics might argue slightly undermines his reliability as a witness but no real evidence exists that Cook did reach Mount McKinley's summit. The consensus today is that he went so far up the mountain and then faked photographs of a much smaller peak to make it look as if he'd achieved his goal.) Claiming to have reached the North Pole when he hadn't was, of course, even more of a dastardly act than claiming to have climbed the highest mountain in North America when he hadn't and Cook vigorously defended the truth of what he had said. 'I stand the most shamefully abused man in the history of exploration,' he wrote when critics pointed out the flimsiness or indeed non-existence of the evidence he was offering that he had reached the pole. However, he lost the battle of words with Peary's supporters. It was a defeat that he undoubtedly deserved. Cook had not done what he said he had done. Not long after Cook made his claims about the pole, a journalist wrote of him that, 'He will count for ever among the greatest impostors of the world. That and not the discovery of the North Pole shall be his claim to immortality.' More than a century later, this still seems the most succinct and truthful statement about Frederick Cook and his status as a polar explorer.

Peary won the battle with Cook. While he was feted for the rest of his life as the man who first made it to the North Pole, his rival was dismissed by nearly everybody as a fraud and crook. It now seems almost certain that Peary himself was guilty of misleading the public. He could not have travelled the distances after he left Bartlett on his polar journey that he recorded any more than he could have achieved those he noted in his 1906 'Furthest North' trip. He may have come close to the pole but he did not actually reach it. Both Peary and Cook lied and misrepresented what they had done. Despite what most people believed for many years, nobody reached the North Pole in either 1908 or 1909.

The Race for the South Pole

The Discovery Expedition: Scott's First Voyage to the Antarctic

Robert Falcon Scott was born in Devon in 1868. His father John owned a brewery in Plymouth and the family, although it was to have its financial problems in later years, was comfortably off. Earlier generations of Scotts had served in both the army and the navy and it was decided that Robert Falcon, always known as 'Con' within the family, would follow in the tradition. He began his career at the age of thirteen as a cadet on the training ship HMS *Britannia*. After leaving *Britannia*, he served, first as a midshipman and then as a sub-lieutenant and a lieutenant, on a number of ships around the world. In 1891, he decided to train as a torpedo officer and, in that capacity, he spent much of the 1890s stationed in the Mediterranean and with the Channel Squadron. Scott was seen as a highly competent, if not brilliant, officer and, apart from an unfortunate incident in 1893 when a torpedo boat under his command ran aground, his career seemed to be making slow but solid progress. By the end of the decade, however, the circumstances of the Scott family had changed dramatically. John Scott, after a series of financial disasters, had died and so too had one of his sons. The burden of supporting his mother and sisters fell on Con. He needed to seek out promotion and a higher profile within the Navy. The British National Antarctic Expedition which had just been announced seemed to offer opportunities for both.

Unlike some Antarctic explorers, Scott had no ambitions cherished since childhood to make his name in the icy wastelands of the Far South. 'I may as well confess at once,' he wrote in his book *The Voyage of the Discovery*, 'that I had no predilection for Polar exploration.' If it had not been for fate and a chance encounter with an important mentor, he might well have spent his career as a relatively undistinguished naval officer, untroubled by fame. The mentor was Sir Clements Markham, President of the Royal Geographical Society between 1888 and 1900 and the man more than any other responsible for the renewal of British interest in polar exploration at the end of the nineteenth century. Markham had first taken note of Scott when, as a midshipman serving in the West Indies, the future explorer had won a sailing race. Eleven years later, with the British National Antarctic Expedition in preparation as a joint venture by the RGS and the Royal Society, Scott and Markham bumped into one another in a London street and the older man persuaded Scott to apply for the job of leading it. Possibly to his surprise, Scott was given command.

The organisation of such an expedition was a time-consuming business and it was more than two years after the meeting with Markham in a London street that the *Discovery* expedition finally left British waters on 6 August 1901. Although there had been some disagreement over the division of responsibilities between Scott and the proposed leader of the scientific contingent, the matter had been settled in Scott's favour and spirits were high aboard the ship. Not even the death of a seaman, who fell from the top of the mainmast while the *Discovery* was in harbour at New Zealand, could dampen the enthusiasm that Scott and the men with him felt for their expedition.

One minor irritant in time to come, however, was the Scottish scientist William Speirs Bruce, who had experience of sailing in both the Arctic and the Antarctic and had expressed an interest in joining Scott's expedition. He and Markham had fallen out and

Bruce was not invited to join the *Discovery*. He then took what, in Markham's eyes, was the unforgivable step of organising his own expedition. He even had the gall to name it the Scottish National Antarctic Expedition in explicit rivalry with Scott's expedition. The president of the RGS was outraged by what he saw as Bruce's ungentlemanly behaviour but the Scotsman sailed south in the *Scotia* fifteen months after the *Discovery* had left Britain and the two expeditions were later in Antarctica at the same time. The Scottish expedition carried out valuable scientific work, the full significance of which has only been appreciated in recent decades, but Markham made sure that it received precious little public recognition when it returned in the summer of 1904.

It was not just Bruce who was threatening to steal Scott's thunder. There were other expeditions in the Antarctic at much the same time as his. Thanks to the enthusiastic advocacy of Clements Markham and similar figures in other countries, polar exploration was beginning to be seen as inextricably linked to national prestige. The Germans wanted a share in any glory that was going and Erich von Drygalski, a veteran of several Arctic journeys, led an expedition that set sail from Kiel in the same month that the *Discovery* left England. Heading south from the Kerguelen Islands, Drygalski's ship the *Gauss* spent months trapped in the ice but emerged in February 1903 with enough scientific material to keep its leader busy in publishing it for the next twenty-five years. The Finnish-Swedish geologist Otto Nordenskjöld, whose uncle had been the first to navigate the Northeast Passage, sailed with a number of scientific colleagues on board a ship called the *Antarctic*, captained by an old Antarctic hand, Carl Larsen. They were left to winter amidst the ice and carry out scientific research. Plans went disastrously wrong. The *Antarctic* sank as it was returning to pick up Nordenskjöld and the men of the expedition were stranded for many months on two separate islands before they could be rescued. Jean-Baptiste Charcot, the son of a famous neurologist whose work was a major influence on Sigmund Freud, led a French expedition which charted several hundred miles of previously unknown Antarctic coastline in 1904 and 1905. However, it was Scott's expedition which was to capture most of the headlines, at least in the English-speaking world.

The roll call of names on the *Discovery* expedition includes many that are now famous in polar history. From Scott's perspective, perhaps the most important addition to his personnel was Edward Wilson who was to become his great friend and closest ally on both his expeditions. Wilson was born in Cheltenham in 1872, the son of a doctor and his wife, and was fascinated by natural history from an early age. He read Natural Sciences at Cambridge and then studied to become a doctor but a bout of tuberculosis, from which he had only just recovered, had delayed his qualification. Now he was to bring his skills in medicine, natural history and as an artist to Scott's party. Other participants in the *Discovery* expedition, including Frank Wild, William Lashly, Thomas Crean and Edgar Evans, had their roles, often significant, to play in the future of polar exploration. The most familiar name of all, however, is that of Ernest Shackleton, Third Officer on the ship. Shackleton was born in February 1874 in a small village in County Kildare, Ireland and moved to London with his family when he was ten. After schooling at Dulwich College, he became a merchant navy officer and served on the Union-Castle line. Through a friend whose father was one of its chief financial backers, he heard of the British National Antarctic Expedition and applied to join it. He was destined to become one of the great figures in the Heroic Age of Polar Exploration.

Scott sailed into the Ross Sea and, in February 1902, established his base at what came to be known as Hut Point on an island connected by ice to nearby Victoria Land. From there it was hoped that there would be access to a route southwards to the pole. Before any polar journey could begin, however, the darkness of the long winter had to pass and Scott's men settled down to endure it as best they could.

On 2 November Scott was finally able to set off on the long-planned march southwards. Accompanying him were Wilson, Shackleton and twenty-two dogs. Progress was slow and food for both men and animals was soon a problem. By December, the men were finding it necessary to kill the weakest of the dogs in order to feed the others. By Christmas Day, when Shackleton attempted to raise some seasonal cheer with a Christmas pudding that he had brought along, wrapped in one of his socks, it was clear that there was no chance of travelling very much further pole-wards. On the very last day of the year, with most of the dogs dead and the three men suffering from frostbite, snow-blindness and the beginnings of scurvy, they reached their furthest point south at 82° 17' and turned back towards the *Discovery*. They had succeeded in travelling 300 miles further south than anyone had ever done but they were still nearly 500 miles from the pole. On the return journey all three men were in a poor condition but Shackleton fared worse than his companions. For long periods of time he was unable to help in pulling the sledges (all the dogs were now gone) and, according to Scott, he had to be occasionally carried on one of them. Shackleton later indignantly denied that this was the case but there is no doubt that he was in very bad shape for most of the return journey. When the three men finally made it back to their winter quarters at McMurdo Sound at the beginning of February 1903, they were all suffering badly but it was only Shackleton who had to be sent home on the relief ship *Morning*. It was a humiliation which Shackleton bitterly resented and which he blamed on Scott as much as the Antarctic conditions. It was to shape his future relations with his fellow explorer and his own future career.

The *Discovery* was to stay in Antarctica for another year and there were to be further sledging journeys. Scott, Lashly and Edgar Evans headed westwards from the base camp and became the first men to venture on to the polar plateau. However, it was the trip to the Farthest South that caught the public's imagination. Shackleton had already been surprised by the attention he had received on returning to Britain. When Scott returned home in the autumn of 1904, he found that, despite the failure to reach the pole, he was still considered a hero. Banquets were given, lectures addressed to packed audiences and the king himself invited him to Balmoral to hear stories of his exploits first-hand.

Farthest South: Shackleton's Expedition of 1909

There was clearly unfinished business in Antarctica for many of those who had already been there. The Frenchman Charcot returned south on his charmingly named ship the *Pourquoi Pas?* ('Why Not?') between 1908 and 1910 and added further discoveries to those he had made several years earlier. Most significantly, Ernest Shackleton, still brooding over the circumstances in which his previous Antarctic trip had ended, was champing at the bit, desperate to go back. With the financial support of a Scottish industrialist named William Beardmore (whose reward was later to have one of the world's largest glaciers named after him), he was finally able to get his plans off the ground. On 11 August 1907, his ship the *Nimrod* sailed from England and, after a stopover in New Zealand, arrived in Antarctic waters in January 1908.

Shackleton had made some kind of commitment not to trespass on what Scott saw as his own territory around McMurdo Sound and had originally intended to land in King Edward VII Land, named during the *Discovery* expedition but visited only briefly for a pioneering balloon flight on the continent. When the *Nimrod* arrived at what was known as Balloon Bight, however, Shackleton found that parts of the ice barrier had broken away since his earlier visit and it was impossible to establish camp there. The only safe place to put his base, he decided, was where Scott had been, although he tried to keep his promise to the older explorer by avoiding Hut

Point. (His scruples proved pointless. Scott was furious when he heard, although it is not only difficult to see what other option Shackleton had, it is also difficult to see how Scott could believe that certain areas in Antarctica somehow 'belonged' to him.)

There were two major journeys on the *Nimrod* expedition. One was the scientific trip by Edgeworth David, Douglas Mawson and Alistair Mackay who succeeded in reaching the South Magnetic Pole on 16 January 1909. The other, and the one that history has remembered so much better, was Shackleton's own journey south in an attempt to reach the pole. He set off on 19 October 1908. With him were three men. Yorkshireman Frank Wild had been an able seaman on the *Discovery* expedition and was to become Shackleton's most trusted subordinate; Eric Marshall was a Cambridge-educated surgeon whom Shackleton had persuaded to join him in the journey south; and Jameson Adams, the second in command of the *Nimrod* expedition, had left the Royal Navy Reserve to volunteer for the expedition. The party's first aim was to pass the Farthest South mark that Shackleton had reached in the company of Scott and Wilson six years earlier. This was achieved on 26 November. The second was to get off the Great Ice Barrier (now known as the Ross Ice Shelf), climb the vast mountain range that confronted them and make it on to the polar plateau, something that Shackleton had been unable to do when travelling with Scott and Wilson. A giant glacier (the Beardmore Glacier), running up through the mountains, offered them the way.

Once on the plateau, they hoped that their journey would become easier but new problems arose. Supplies were running low, temperatures were plunging and man-hauling the sledges became ever more demanding. As Shackleton eventually noted, 'We have shot our bolt...' Exhausted, hungry and suffering from altitude sickness and the beginnings of scurvy, they had come as far as they could. When they reached their furthest point south at 88° 23' on 9 January 1909, the four men were less than 100 nautical miles from the pole. Shackleton's decision to turn back is arguably the bravest of his career. The temptation to push on and risk everything in getting to his goal must have been enormous but, had he done so, he and his men would almost certainly have perished. They would have been heroes but dead heroes. Instead, Shackleton (unlike so many of his fellow explorers in both the Antarctic and the Arctic) took the sensible option and turned for home. 'Our food lies ahead,' Shackleton wrote with forgivable melodrama, 'and death stalks us from behind.' Rations were drastically reduced as they made their ever more difficult return journey. Gaunt and half-starving, they arrived back at the base on the last day of February. They were close to the end but they were also in luck. The following day the *Nimrod* arrived to pick them up.

Shackleton returned to England to find himself a popular hero. He was feted, knighted and turned into a wax sculpture in Madame Tussauds. He may have put Scott's nose out of joint by basing himself in McMurdo Sound and Sir Clements Markham took to referring to him in private as 'that ungrateful cad' but the public loved him. The onus was now on Scott to go one better than his rival and reach the pole.

The Terra Nova: The Tragedy of Scott's Second Expedition

In the years since returning from the Antarctic, Scott had become a public figure who was recognised by the average man in the street. He had married Kathleen Bruce, a sculptor from a more bohemian background than those usually associated with the wives of naval officers. Ten years younger than Scott, she had studied in Paris where she had known Rodin and her social circle in London included the likes of Max Beerbohm and JM Barrie. She met the polar hero at a party given by the sister of the late Aubrey Beardsley, a social event at which she would have probably been more comfortable than her husband-to-be. However, despite his marriage, Scott's desire to renew his career as an explorer was still strong and, some months after Shackleton's triumphal return from the *Nimrod* expedition, he was able to announce plans for his own second expedition.

The process of gathering together the personnel began. Edward 'Teddy' Evans, who had been one of the officers on the relief ship which had supported the *Discovery* expedition, was said to be planning his own Antarctic expedition. Scott met with him and offered him the opportunity to be his second in command which Evans accepted. Edward Wilson was appointed head of the scientific party which included the geologist Frank Debenham, later to be the first director of the Scott Polar Research Institute in Cambridge, Raymond Priestley, another geologist with a distinguished career ahead of him, and George Simpson who was to become the first and longest-serving director of the Meteorological Office. (There can be no doubting Scott's genuine commitment to scientific research. Debenham wrote in a letter home that 'the interest he takes in our scientific work is immense'.) A ship, the *Terra Nova*, was found and purchased. It was to be manned by mainly Royal Navy seamen, some of them familiar names from the *Discovery* – Lashly, Crean, Edgar Evans. Finance came from a mixture of government money and private subscription.

The *Terra Nova* sailed from Cardiff on 15 June 1910 and arrived in Antarctica just over six months later. After some debate, Scott chose a site on a cape he named Evans after his second in command as his main base and the men unloaded the supplies that were to feed them and the assorted dogs, ponies and sledges which were, they hoped, going to carry some of them to the pole. There were to be a series of different expeditions within the main expedition during the time Scott and his men were in Antarctica. One of the classic accounts of polar exploration is *The Worst Journey in the World* by Apsley

Cherry-Garrard, who served on the *Terra Nova*. Those who have not read the book but know that it is about Scott's second expedition might assume that it takes its title from the doomed journey to the pole. In fact, 'the worst journey in the world' refers to an earlier trip on which Cherry-Garrard, accompanied by Edward Wilson and 'Birdie' Bowers, travelled from the expedition's base at Cape Evans to Cape Crozier. The journey was made in the midst of an Antarctic winter, in complete darkness and in temperatures that fell to more than 70° below zero. Its aim was to gather penguin eggs. There was also to be a 'Northern Party' under the command of an officer named Victor Campbell which was to explore and carry out scientific work from a base on Cape Adare. There were to be geological trips led by Debenham. However, in the public's estimation, the success or failure of Scott's expedition would be judged by whether or not he made it to the pole.

The eventual plan for the pole he devised became an elaborate exercise in logistics in which men, dogs, ponies and motorised sledges all had to be coordinated and combined. The journey, with support teams turning back one by one as the days passed and the miles were covered, would culminate in a team of four men making the final dash to the pole. The first task was to lay the depots for the polar party – the stores of supplies which would enable them to return safely – and a group of men set out to do that at the end of January 1911. The ponies which had been brought soon proved troublesome. They simply could not travel well in the conditions and Lawrence Oates, the laconic army officer who was in charge of them, argued that they should be killed for meat so that the party could make its way further south to lay the last depot. Scott disagreed and, in the end, One Ton Depot was situated thirty miles nearer to the main base than had been originally intended. It was to prove a crucial distance.

The men now retired to Cape Evans to see out the winter. It was not until 24 October that Teddy Evans, Lashly and two other men set off with the motor sledges and they were followed just over a week later by the main group. Almost as soon as the journey began it became clear that the motor sledges were not going to work. They were abandoned at the beginning of November. The men continued to cross the Great Ice Barrier, laying further depots as they did so. One party turned back in the midst of the Barrier; another at the foot of the Beardmore Glacier which Shackleton had shown provided a route on to the polar plateau; another turned north soon after they had reached the plateau.

On 3 January 1912, the last eight men reached 87° 32'. With about 150 miles to go to the pole it was time for the last support party to turn back. It was at this point that Scott made one of the more debatable and controversial decisions of the whole expedition. He announced that 'Birdie' Bowers would join the polar party. This meant that Teddy Evans now had to return with only two men, Tom Crean and William Lashly. All three were hugely disappointed not to have been picked for the last dash to the pole and, because all the planning had been predicated on four-man sledge teams, their return was not easy. Evans collapsed with scurvy and his companions had to haul him on the sledge. When they were still more than 35 miles from home, they could go no further. Leaving Lashly and Evans behind, Crean, near to collapse himself, had to stagger on alone to the base to fetch help. As for the newly augmented polar party, the decision meant that man-hauling was easier with five men rather than four but that there would be extra, unplanned demand on rations and fuel on the return journey.

On 17 January 1912, Scott and his four companions attained their goal but they had arrived second. A Norwegian party under the leadership of Roald Amundsen had been there a month before. 'The Pole. Yes, but under very different circumstances from those expected,' Scott wrote dispiritedly in his diary. 'We have had a horrible day... Great God! this is an awful place and terrible enough for us to have laboured to it without the reward of priority.' All that could be done was to make further readings to ensure that they had indeed reached their goal, pose miserably for a few photographs and then set off on the long journey back to their home base at Cape Evans. It soon became clear that the going would be very difficult indeed.

The first to die was Edgar Evans who collapsed, unable to continue, on 16 February. He may well have been suffering from concussion from an earlier fall but the loss of Evans, who had always seemed such a tower of physical strength, must have disturbed the others greatly. They continued to trudge through the white wilderness, hauling their sledges behind them, but doubts about making it back must have been in the backs of all their minds.

Oates had been suffering more than the others from frostbite and had been unable to pull his weight with the sledges for some time. By 17 March he had had enough and realised that he was holding the others back. His famous act of self-sacrifice is recorded by Scott in his diary in these words: 'He slept through the night before last, hoping not to wake; but he woke in the morning – yesterday. It was blowing a blizzard. He said, "I am just going outside and may be some time." He went out into the blizzard and we have not seen him since.'

The others managed to stagger another twenty miles. They were not far from One Ton Depot but they could go no further. Trapped within their tent, Scott, Bowers and Wilson could only wait to die. 'Every day we have been ready to start for our depot 11 miles away,' Scott wrote in the last entry in his journal, 'but outside the door of the tent it remains a scene of whirling drift. I do not think we can hope for any better things now. We shall stick it out to the end, but we are getting weaker, of course, and the end cannot be far. It seems a pity, but I do not think I can write more.' Underneath these words is a final scrawled entry which reads: 'For God's sake look after our people.' The bodies of the three men were found by a search party eight months later.

Scott's reputation has fluctuated wildly in the century since his death. When the news of his death and those of his companions first reached home, he was hailed as a gallant hero, cheated by fate of the prize that should have been his. For decades, in Britain and the Empire, this was how his story was presented. With the disappearance of the Empire, the glamour of other imperial heroes swiftly vanished but Scott continued to be admired as an exemplar of courage and endurance. It was only in the late 1970s, and particularly with the publication of Roland Huntford's revisionist biography *Scott and Amundsen*, that a different portrait of the man emerged. Huntford's Scott was little more than a vain and blinkered fool who made bad decisions, antagonised his men and led a number of them to their entirely avoidable deaths. He was not so much a hero, more a buffoon and entirely undeserving of admiration.

Shackleton took Scott's place as the most admired of English-speaking polar explorers. In the last decade or so, the pendulum has again swung in Scott's favour. Sir Ranulph Fiennes (presumably a man who knows something about the subject) sprang to his defence in a 2003 biography and other recent biographers have tried to counterbalance Huntford's thoroughgoing debunking of the myth. Perhaps most importantly, new research has shown, very nearly conclusively, that weather conditions were, as Scott claimed in his diaries, particularly bad in 1912 in the area of Antarctica where he and his men were struggling to get back to their base. His polar journey might have been better planned and there is no doubt that Scott was a difficult leader who made some questionable decisions at crucial moments in the expedition. However, even if he had been a paragon amongst commanders, the final, fatal outcome of his journey might well have been the same.

The Triumph of Amundsen

Antarctica was not short of visitors at the time of Scott's ill-fated expedition. Led by an army lieutenant named Nobu Shirase, the

Japanese Antarctic Expedition sailed from Yokohama in November 1910 with the intention of conquering the pole. After an abortive attempt to reach Antarctica and an enforced return to Australia in the early part of 1911, Shirase's men finally made it to the Antarctic mainland in January of 1912. By this time, Scott was staring defeat in the face and Amundsen was most of the way back to his base. Despite newspaper reports in Sydney that the Japanese had taken an oath to reach the pole or commit *hara-kiri*, Shirase very sensibly decided that such extreme measures were unnecessary. He contented himself with an eight-day 'dash patrol' into the interior and further exploration of the coastline of King Edward VII Land. The Japanese did, however, encounter Amundsen's ship, the *Fram*, which was awaiting his return from the pole. Far from civilisation, the Japanese and the Norwegians entertained one another to dinner although lack of a common language severely restricted conversation. Meanwhile a German explorer named Wilhelm Filchner had entered the Weddell Sea on the opposite side of the continent in late 1911. His ship, the *Deutschland*, soon became caught in the pack ice. He and his men, unable to land on the ice shelf, were obliged to overwinter on the ship and it was not until September 1912 that they were released from the pack ice's grip.

However, Scott's greatest rivals were the Norwegians whose expedition Nobu Shirase's men encountered. Their leader, already renowned for his Arctic exploits, was Roald Amundsen. Since his triumph in traversing the Northwest Passage, the Norwegian had been casting around for another project which would add to his already substantial reputation. His original plan was to reach the North Pole not the South Pole but, when word came that Peary was claiming to have achieved that goal, Amundsen secretly made the decision that his only hope for further polar glory now lay in sailing southwards. On 3 June 1910, he left Oslo on his ship the *Fram*, which had been designed and built for Nansen nearly twenty years earlier. Most of his men still believed that they were destined for the North Pole and it was only when they reached Madeira that they were told of the change of plan. At the same time Amundsen despatched a telegram to Australia for Scott to peruse when he arrived there. 'Beg leave to inform you *Fram* proceeding Antarctica', it read.

Amundsen made no further stops after Madeira. At the beginning of 1911, the *Fram* arrived at the Bay of Whales, an inlet of the Ross Sea which was situated at the opposite end of the Great Ice Barrier from Scott's camp and which had been named by Shackleton on his *Nimrod* expedition. (Indeed, Shackleton had considered using the Bay of Whales as his base in 1908 but had decided it was too dangerous. Amundsen seems not to have had such qualms.) Amundsen's men, who included Hjalmar Johansen, Nansen's companion on the Farthest North journey in 1895, began to unload the supplies and build their base which they called *Framheim*. Depot-laying journeys were made southwards and then the Norwegians settled in to endure the long polar winter.

As the first signs of spring appeared, Amundsen was anxious to be on his way. A premature attempt on the pole in September ended in near disaster and a severe quarrel with Johansen who had the temerity, as Amundsen saw it, to question his leadership skills in front of others. (Johansen's reward was to be barred from the final polar journey and virtually written out of the history of the expedition. Sent home to Norway in 'disgrace', he suffered from alcoholism and depression and shot himself in an Oslo park in 1913.) The Norwegians set off again on 19 October. Unlike Scott, with his complicated mishmash of transport methods, Amundsen had committed himself to one, simple means of getting to the pole. The men would travel on skis and dogs would pull sledges with the supplies. As dogs weakened, they would be shot and fed both to the animals that survived and to the men. Even his rival, when he heard of the plan, half-acknowledged its strength. 'If he gets to the Pole, it must be before we do,' Scott wrote in a letter, 'as he is bound to travel fast with dogs.' He was right. Amundsen and his four companions (champion skier Olav Bjaaland, Helmer Hanssen who had been on the journey through the Northwest Passage, Oscar Wisting and the expert dog driver Sverre Hassel) made good time. They reached the edge of the ice shelf in the middle of November and, like Shackleton some years earlier, faced the problem of climbing the mountains ahead of them and getting themselves on to the polar plateau. Again like the Irish explorer, they found a glacier (named the Axel Heiberg Glacier after one of the expedition's main sponsors) which gave them access to the plateau. Once they made it to the top of the glacier, they slaughtered the majority of the dogs at a camp they called the Butcher's Shop and moved ever nearer their goal. Passing Shackleton's furthest point south on 8 December, they reached the pole six days later. After spending the next few days making a series of sextant readings and calculations to confirm that they had indeed achieved ninety degrees south, the Norwegians set off for Framheim. The return journey went as smoothly as the outer journey, if not more so, and they made it back to their base on 25 January 1912. Eight days earlier Scott and his companions had arrived at the pole to find the unmistakeable evidence that they had come second in the race.

Why exactly did Amundsen succeed in his polar mission and Scott fail in his? As we have seen, many of the criticisms levelled at Scott in the last thirty years have been unfair. He was not the blinkered fool that some biographers have tried to depict. However, he was not as clear-sighted about getting to the pole as his rival was. Scott, arguably to his credit, was interested in much more than just the race to the pole. The *Terra Nova* expedition was the most scientifically sophisticated and well-equipped expedition to have visited Antarctica up to that point and this was reflected in the vast volumes of scientific research from it that were published when it returned sadly home. Amundsen, by contrast, was single-minded in his pursuit of the pole. He had worked out a means of reaching his goal that was simple and straightforward where Scott's was complicated and often difficult to put into practice. It was not so surprising that the Norwegian won the race.

The Arctic 1910–1960

Amundsen by Land, Sea and Air

In the years immediately following the disputed journeys of both Peary and Cook, other Arctic expeditions were mounted. Knud Rasmussen, born in Greenland of a Danish father and a part-Inuit mother, had been exploring the remoter areas of his native country and the richness of Inuit culture for some years. In 1912, he embarked on the first of what were called the Thule expeditions which were to continue until his death in 1933.

Several other expeditions were Russian and all of these ended in disaster. In 1912, Vladimir Rusanov, a geologist with an interest in the mineralogical potential of the Russian Arctic, embarked on an ill-judged attempt to sail through what was once known as the Northeast Passage to the Pacific. His ship and those on board, including Alexander Kuchin who had been the only non-Norwegian member of Amundsen's South Pole expedition, disappeared somewhere in the Kara Sea, off the northern coast of Siberia. The same year saw a naval officer named Georgy Brusilov make a similar attempt to take his ship, the *St Anna*, from west to east along his country's Arctic coastline. Trapped in the pack ice, Brusilov and his men succumbed to disease and hunger. After a despairing march southwards, two survivors reached safety. No trace of the rest of the *St Anna's* crew was found until a handful of relics turned up on the shores of Franz Josef Land in 2010. The only one of these ill-fated Russian expeditions to have the pole as its target was led by Georgy Sedov, a gifted man who had risen from a poor background to become a naval officer. He had already been on two state-sponsored Arctic expeditions when he suggested a mission to reach the pole. It was turned down by the government but he raised private funds to take him north. The expedition was soon in difficulties. Although suffering from scurvy and painfully aware that his chances of reaching the pole were almost zero, Sedov insisted on making the attempt. On 15 February 1914, he set off northwards with two companions but died before he could make much progress.

Meanwhile in the West, the Canadian government sponsored an expedition to explore the still unmapped regions of the country. Unfortunately, the expedition resulted in death, disaster and bitter recrimination. Its leader was Vilhjalmur Stefansson, originally known as William Stephenson, who had been born in Manitoba in 1879 to recent immigrants from Iceland. After reverting to an Icelandic version of his name as a young man, Stefansson was already an experienced traveller in the Arctic by the time he proposed explorations north and west of already charted land to discover what might lie there. He and the men he recruited set off from British Columbia in June 1913 aboard the *Karluk*, a refitted whaler. By September, the ship was trapped in the ice north of Alaska and Stefansson announced that he was leaving her, with five companions, to hunt for caribou. Almost as soon as he left, the ice in which the *Karluk* was trapped began to move and the ship drifted inexorably westwards. Stefannsson was never able to rejoin her and she was now solely under the command of her captain, Robert Bartlett, veteran of three expeditions with Robert Peary. In January 1914, the *Karluk* sank under the ice and most of the people on board were stranded on Wrangel Island off the northern Siberian coast. Bartlett and an Inuit hunter made an epic journey back to Alaska to summon assistance but eleven lives had been lost by the time he could return. Stefansson, who had already reached safety, had resumed his explorations and they continued for some years. He did indeed find new lands as he had originally intended but his reputation was badly damaged by what had happened and by the suspicions that he had deliberately abandoned the *Karluk*. (It was not improved by a later fatal fiasco in 1921 when Stefansson encouraged four young men to land on Wrangel Island in an attempt to claim it for Canada. All of them died.)

Sedov's doomed expedition and the ill-fated voyage of the *Karluk* marked the end of an era. In August 1914, the First World War began and the ambitions of polar explorers seemed petty and irrelevant in the context of global conflict. Their sufferings and sacrifices in the past were now overshadowed by the colossal loss of life in the fields of Flanders and elsewhere. It was only when the war to end all wars was finally over that public fascination with Arctic exploration was renewed. By this time, new technologies which had come of age in the war could be employed in the Far North. The aeroplane and the airship arrived in the Arctic.

Richard E Byrd came from a family which could trace its American origins right back to the earliest days of European settlement. (He even claimed John Rolfe and the Native American princess Pocahontas as his ancestors.) His father was a leading politician in Virginia and his brother became a senator and governor of his home state. Richard Byrd himself joined the US Navy and became a passionate enthusiast for flying. After serving in the First World War, he turned his attention to polar flight. Sailing on a ship captained by Robert Bartlett, the hero of the *Karluk* expedition, he arrived at Spitsbergen with fellow pilot Floyd Bennett in late April 1926. Just over a week later, Byrd and Bennett took off in a Fokker Trimotor and headed in the direction of the North Pole. In little more than fifteen hours they were back, claiming that they had, according to their readings, reached the pole and circled around it before flying back to the base in Spitsbergen. Had the two men really made it to the pole? People at the time certainly thought so. Byrd was given a tickertape welcome when he returned to New York and was hailed as an authentic American hero. However some experts, then and since, have had their doubts. Could the Fokker plane have travelled the distance in the time that it had been in the air? Were Byrd's navigational readings accurate? Perhaps the two Americans had only come within fifty miles of the pole but not actually gone the full distance before turning back.

Whatever the truth of the matter, it was certainly the case that there was plenty of activity in the Arctic air in the late 1920s. The Australian-born Hubert Wilkins, who had worked as a photographer on earlier Arctic expeditions and travelled as an ornithologist on Shackleton's final voyage, had long been planning a headline-grabbing exploit. After two false starts in previous years, Wilkins and his pilot Carl Ben Eielson succeeded in flying from Alaska to Spitsbergen, from America to Europe via the Arctic, in April 1928, two years after Byrd and Bennett's possible polar flight. However, Byrd's greatest rival for acclaim was someone who was in Spitsbergen at the very time he was, and was already one of the most famous explorers in the world.

Since the end of the First World War, Roald Amundsen, conqueror of the South Pole, had been involved in an extended attempt to sail a ship, the *Maud*, through the Northeast Passage and, perhaps, do what Nansen had failed to do nearly thirty years earlier – drift in an ice-trapped vessel across the North Pole. By 1923, realising that the future of polar exploration was in the air rather than the sea, Amundsen had turned his attentions from ship to plane. With a pilot named Oskar Omdal, he tried to fly from Alaska to Spitsbergen across the pole but failed. Two years later, with the support of the wealthy American Lincoln Ellsworth and the assistance of pilot and fellow-countryman Hjalmar Riiser-Larsen, Amundsen mounted another airborne attempt on the pole. They disappeared over the horizon in two Dornier flying boats and were out of contact with the rest of the world for more than three weeks. On 15 June 1925, as the obituarists were preparing their newspaper columns, one of the

Dorniers returned, crash-landing in the sea off Spitsbergen. The planes had made it to 87° 14′ before engine trouble had forced them on to the ice. Eventually, all the members of the expedition had been forced to cram themselves into one plane which had limped its way back to safety.

Despite these setbacks, Amundsen was still determined to reach the pole by air. He now decided that an airship was the answer and contacted the Italian expert on airships, Umberto Nobile, to ask him to provide one. Nobile agreed to modify an airship he had already built and rename it the *Norge* but he wanted to come along for the ride. He was recruited to the mission. He turned out to be a difficult colleague and, by the time the airship arrived in Spitsbergen in April 1926, relations between Amundsen and Nobile and between the Norwegians and the Italians in the extended expedition were strained. The American Ellsworth whose money was making everything possible was an uneasy peacemaker. With squabbling between the various members of the team still in full swing (Amundsen was later to claim that Nobile had been a menace to the safety of the airship), the *Norge* took off from Spitsbergen on 11 May and headed for Alaska. Its route took it over the pole the following day (Ellsworth's birthday) and an assortment of national flags was dropped onto the snow and ice. According to Amundsen, a previous arrangement had been made to use only small flags but the Italians broke it by throwing out a banner so large that it was very nearly caught up in the airship's propellers. The Norwegian was furious but the mission had been successful. When the *Norge* landed in Alaska on the morning of 14 May, it had achieved all that had been planned for it.

Previous claims to the pole – by Peary, Cook and Byrd in his flight only a short time before the *Norge*'s journey – have all been mired in controversy and dispute. There is no doubt that Amundsen and his crew of various bickering nationalities *did* fly over the pole. If the earlier claims are false, then Amundsen and Oscar Wisting, who was on the airship with him, were not only among the first men to reach the South Pole. They were also among the first men to reach ninety degrees north.

Umberto Nobile and the Italia Expedition

Meanwhile Umberto Nobile was not finished with the Arctic. After building another airship, which he named *Italia*, Nobile took it north with plans to make a series of flights, culminating in a journey to the pole. On 23 May 1928, the *Italia* set off for the pole and reached it without difficulty the following day. Problems occurred, however, on the return journey and the airship crashed north of Spitsbergen on 25 May. Its gondola broke into bits and the men inside it were stranded on the ice. Nobile himself was badly injured. The airship's envelope, the gas-filled outer structure, was freed of the gondola's weight and drifted off into the Arctic skies. Six men trapped in it were never seen again. The survivors on the ice established some sort of camp and began to radio for help. Their SOS signals did not get through but, back at the *Italia*'s base, it was soon clear that something had gone terribly wrong with the airship.

Within days, the first plane had flown out to search for it and over the next few weeks, a series of rescue missions was organised to try to locate Nobile and his men. Even Roald Amundsen, who had disagreed so profoundly with the Italian and found him so difficult a colleague, volunteered to join the search. On 17 June, he boarded a plane flying towards Spitsbergen. It disappeared the following day. Parts of the aircraft were later found off the north Norwegian coast but the body of the legendary explorer, the man who had first reached the South Pole, was never found. Three days later the stranded Italians were spotted from the air. A plane landed to pick up the injured Nobile but initially he refused to leave without his men and had to be more or less forced aboard against his will. When the pilot tried to return to rescue the other survivors, after taking Nobile to safety, he crashed his own aircraft. A fellow pilot had to rescue him. Eventually all the Italians were taken on board by a Russian ice-breaker.

In 1930, fourteen intrepid young Britons, led by the charismatic Gino Watkins, set out to investigate the possibilities for air travel between Europe and America via the northern polar regions. The British Arctic Air Route Expedition endured conditions almost as bad as those that had plagued some of the pioneering Arctic explorers. One of its members, Augustine Courtauld, volunteered to spend time alone on the Greenland ice cap making meteorological observations. He ended up trapped there for five months, spending much of his solitary exile from his fellows in total darkness, pinned down in his icy shelter by the most extreme forms imaginable of the weather he had come to study. Astonishingly, when he was eventually rescued, he had somehow managed to retain his sanity. Courtauld's ordeal was the worst of those Watkins's men had to endure but others experienced danger and disaster on land and in the air. The expedition, however, was one of the last of its kind. Watkins himself, who was something of a throwback to the heroic age of polar exploration, died in a kayaking accident off the coast of Greenland in 1932. He was aged only 25.

In 1931, Hubert Wilkins, after leasing an old World War I submarine for the nominal sum of one dollar a year and renaming it the *Nautilus* in imitation of Captain Nemo's vessel in Jules Verne's novel *Twenty Thousand Leagues Under the Sea*, announced that he would travel under the ice to the pole. His plans went badly from the very beginning. A crewman drowned before the *Nautilus* had even left New York harbour. When it made it into the Atlantic, its engines promptly began to fail and, after limping halfway across the ocean, it had to be rescued by a US Navy ship and towed into an Irish port. Repairs were undertaken and, by the end of August, it had reached the Arctic ice. Only when the submarine was about to submerge did the captain notice that the diving planes, which were essential to controlling it under the water, were missing. Amidst suspicions of sabotage, Wilkins tried to salvage something from the wreckage by carrying out a few scientific experiments but even one of the expedition's main sponsors was now proposing that he should give up. 'I most urgently beg of you to return promptly to safety and to defer any further adventure to a more favorable time, and with a better boat,' read a wireless message sent by the newspaper tycoon William Randolph Hearst. Wilkins wisely decided that discretion was the better part of valour and abandoned his plans for the expedition. The unfortunate *Nautilus* was eventually scuttled in a Norwegian fjord in November 1931.

The Soviets by Sea and Air and the Americans Under the Ice

At the same time as Watkins and Wilkins were, in their very different ways, continuing the western tradition of Arctic exploration, the Soviet Union was beginning to show an interest in the Far North. There had been little Russian involvement with the region since the Revolution but a polymath named Otto Schmidt was eager to change that. In 1929, Schmidt led a party of scientists aboard the ice-breaker *Sedov* (named after the naval officer who had died while attempting to reach the pole in 1914) to Franz Josef Land. On his return he was appointed head of the Arctic Institute in Moscow and, in this role, was able to encourage and initiate further Soviet expeditions. In 1932, another ice-breaker, the A *Sibiriyakov*, became the first ship to navigate the Northeast Passage along Russia's northern coastline, from the port of Archangel to the Bering Strait, without overwintering.

Schmidt was on board. He was also the driving force behind another journey the following year, in which the steamship *Chelyuskin* attempted to match the achievement of the *Sibiriyakov*. It nearly did so but, as it approached the last part of the route, it was caught in pack ice and forced ever further away from its goal. After four months trapped in the ice, it was crushed and sank. Those on board, with the exception of one unfortunate who drowned, were able to scramble on to the ice but their ordeal was not yet over. Weeks passed before rescuing aircraft could reach them and even then it took nearly a dozen flights to get everybody to safety. The pilots who flew the rescue missions became the first people to be awarded the title Hero of the Soviet Union, later to be the highest distinction the country could bestow.

Some of those pilots were also active in the sequence of polar flights that were headline news in the Soviet Union in the late 1930s and contributed enormously to the cult of the heroic pilot under Stalin. Meanwhile Otto Schmidt's fertile mind had come up with a new way for Soviet explorers and scientific researchers to investigate the Arctic regions. Drawing on the ideas that had inspired Nansen forty years earlier, Schmidt established North Pole-1, the first of what would be dozens of drifting ice stations (the latest began operations in 2012) which used the natural drift of the ice to carry those on board through the Arctic seas.

After the Second World War, the Soviets continued to invest in expeditions to the North Pole – a Russian party under the leadership of Alexander Kuznetsov landed there from an aircraft in 1948 – but it was the Americans who demonstrated the continuing power of new technology to redefine Arctic travel. Taking the name of the submarine commanded by the enigmatic Captain Nemo in Jules Verne's 1870 novel *Twenty Thousand Leagues Under the Sea*, and echoing that of the ship in which Hubert Wilkins had first attempted to show the possibilities of under-ice travel, the USS *Nautilus* was launched in 1954. The first nuclear-powered submarine, *Nautilus* was able to stay underwater for much longer periods than non-nuclear submarines and eye-catching missions to show off its capacities were soon being sought. No operation was likely to garner more headlines for the submarine than a journey beneath the Arctic ice to the North Pole. Such a voyage would also advertise to the

Russians the potential of the weapons systems *Nautilus* carried. In August 1958, in a mission which the Americans playfully called 'Operation Sunshine', the submarine submerged off the coast of Alaska and headed under the ice to the pole, returning four days later to the waters off Greenland.

Other American submarines followed the *Nautilus*'s example. The USS *Skate*, which had already been there soon after the pioneering submarine in 1958, arrived at the pole again in March 1959. This time it surfaced in order to scatter the ashes of Sir Hubert Wilkins who had died the previous year. In August 1962, the *Skate* went to the pole again, this time in a mini-convoy with the USS *Seadragon*. The two submarines had rendezvoused under the ice two days earlier and they both surfaced together at the pole. The Nuclear Age had well and truly reached the Arctic.

The Antarctic 1912–1960

Australia Advances: Mawson's Expedition

Australia's most famous polar explorer, Douglas Mawson was actually born in Yorkshire in 1882 but his family emigrated to New South Wales when he was a small child. He studied mining engineering at the University of Sydney and became well-known as a geologist while still in his twenties. As we have seen, he first visited the Antarctic as a member of Shackleton's *Nimrod* expedition between 1907 and 1909. He might well have joined Scott's second expedition – he met Scott and had extensive conversations with him – but he wanted to go as chief scientist and Edward Wilson had already been promised that position. He might also have travelled south again with Shackleton who was also proposing a new expedition but this came to nothing. Instead, Mawson ended by leading his own Australian expedition to Antarctica in the busy year of 1912. If Scott and Amundsen's expeditions marked the culmination and conclusion of the Heroic Age of Antarctic exploration, then this Australasian Antarctic Expedition pointed the way forward to a new era in which science would take the lead. It was not without its heroics (and earlier expeditions were certainly not without scientific endeavour) but Mawson's expedition was dominated by science and by scientists as no expedition had previously been. Its leader was, of course, primarily a scientist himself. It left Hobart in Tasmania in December 1911 and, just over a month later, a main base was established at what Mawson called Cape Denison in honour of the businessman Hugh Denison who was one of the expedition's chief financial backers.

Now considered one of the windiest places on the planet, Cape Denison became the expedition's home for the next two years and the starting point for a series of sledging trips to carry out the ambitious plans of exploration Mawson had formulated. Ever a forward thinker, he had also brought a small plane with him, the first aircraft in Antarctica, in the hopes of undertaking aerial exploration but the Vickers monoplane was damaged before it even reached the ice and never worked properly. It was left to men and dogs to carry out the journeys into the unknown, mostly from Cape Denison but a few from another base established further west. By far the most significant of these in terms of its future fame if not its scientific results was known as the Far Eastern Party.

It consisted of Mawson himself, a young British soldier named Belgrave Ninnis whose father had been a member of Nares's Arctic expedition in the 1870s and Xavier Mertz, a Swiss skiing expert, and it set out on 10 November 1912. Its aim was to chart territory to the east of Cape Denison and to collect geological specimens. For a month, all went well but on 14 December tragedy stuck. While Ninnis was crossing a crevasse the snow opened beneath his feet and he fell to his death. The two other men immediately turned for home but a significant part of the supplies and some of the dogs had followed poor Ninnis into the depths of the crevasse. Short of food, Mertz and Mawson were obliged to eat the remaining dogs. What they did not realise, because it was a fact as yet unknown to science, was that dog's liver, which they were forcing down themselves, contained toxic levels of vitamin A. Both men became ill but Mertz, who had eaten more of the liver, had worse symptoms than Mawson. By January, he was in a bad way, suffering from dysentery, loss of skin from his limbs and delirium. On the 8th of that month, after a last bout of raving in which he bit off one of his own fingers, he fell into unconsciousness and died.

Mawson was alone amidst the ice, seriously ill himself, and still 100 miles from safety.

The Australian pushed on but his body was literally falling apart. He was losing skin from his hands and legs, his hair was coming out in clumps and his soles, which had entirely separated from his feet, needed binding back on before he could walk. Throwing away everything inessential apart from some geological specimens and the records of the ill-fated trip, he still struggled to make more than a few miles a day. On several occasions he fell into crevasses but was able somehow to haul himself out and continue. With his food nearly gone, he stumbled across a cairn containing supplies that had been left by those now out searching for him. It enabled him to make one last push for home. On 8 February, exactly a month since Mertz's death had left him as the Far Eastern Party's sole survivor, Mawson reached the hut at Cape Denison. He was so badly reduced by malnutrition and illness as to be unrecognisable. 'My God, which one are you?' are supposed to have been the first words of the first man to see him. The relief ship, the *Aurora*, had sailed for Australia the day before but five men had remained behind on the off chance that members of the Far Eastern Party were still alive. They nursed their leader back to health and all six spent another winter in the Antarctic. Sir Edmund Hillary later called Mawson's journey 'the greatest survival story in the history of exploration'.

Endurance: Imperial Trans-Antarctic Expedition

With the prize of the pole already taken, what was there left for a man like Shackleton to claim? He was not a scientist like Mawson. His expeditions depended on the kind of bold and easily understood goal that would appeal to the general public. He came up with just the kind of headline-catching objective that he needed when, in December 1913, he announced the Imperial Trans-Antarctic Expedition. In what he described, immodestly but not entirely unfairly, as 'the greatest Polar journey ever attempted', he would set out from the shore of the Weddell Sea and, with five companions, cross the continent to the Ross Sea.

The *Endurance* left Britain at the beginning of August 1914, just a few days after war against the Kaiser's Germany was declared. Shackleton, eager to demonstrate his patriotism, was prepared to abandon the expedition and devote its resources to the war effort but he was told to carry on. With Frank Wild, his companion on previous expeditions and on the Farthest South journey of 1909, as his second in command, he sailed for South Georgia where he learned that the pack ice in the Weddell Sea had been particularly thick that year. Shackleton decided none the less to stick to his original plan and pressed on southwards but, by January 1915, the *Endurance* was in the grip of the ice. Not only was it held fast it was also being forced further and further away from the expedition's proposed landing place.

For the next nine months, including the winter months of complete darkness, the ship drifted in the grip of the pack ice. Shackleton and his men, although they made concerted efforts to free it, were eventually obliged to reconcile themselves to being trapped. They could only wait for the ice to begin to break up. Unfortunately, as it did so, it put them in greater danger. The melting floes buffeted and pressurised the *Endurance*, threatening to sink or destroy it. As his vessel was thrown about, Shackleton realised that it was ultimately doomed. On 27 October, he gave the order to abandon ship and the expedition took to the ice. Just over three weeks later the *Endurance* could endure no more and slipped beneath the ice. Shackleton and his men were left on the drifting ice floes. They were carried on them for the next five months, with firm land often in sight but inaccessible. By the beginning of April 1916, as the floes broke up, it was clear that the men could no longer stay where they were and, on the 9th of that month, Shackleton ordered his men aboard three lifeboats that they had rescued from the *Endurance*.

The boats reached Elephant Island, part of the South Shetlands archipelago, in the middle of April. Seeing no hope of rescue and no alternative course of action, Shackleton then set off for South Georgia some 800 nautical miles away, where the whaling station that he had visited in 1914 offered the hope of rescue. Taking five men with him on the lifeboat *James Caird*, he left the rest on Elephant Island under the command of Frank Wild. For sixteen days, Shackleton and his companions battled through fearsome seas in the 23-foot-long boat and eventually made it to South Georgia on 10 May. Unfortunately, they could only land on the opposite side of the island from the whaling station. Two of the *James Caird*'s crew could go no further and were left in a makeshift camp. Together with Frank Worsley, the captain of the lost *Endurance*, and Tom Crean, a veteran of Scott's Antarctic voyages, Shackleton had to make one final effort and trek thirty miles across mountain and glacier to alert the Norwegian whalers to their presence. Once they had done so, the two men on the far side of the island were rescued and, after a delay of some months due to weather conditions, Wild's party on Elephant Island was picked up and returned to civilisation. Despite all the perils and all the misfortunes, there had been no loss of life. The *James Caird*, which had made one of the most extraordinary journeys in polar history, is currently on display in Dulwich College, Shackleton's old school.

Shackleton was to organise one more expedition to Antarctica. Its objectives may not always have been entirely clear and Shackleton may have been pursued by the debts and doubts that had dogged his career but he was still able to attract the attention of press and public. The *Quest*, a converted Norwegian sealer, sailed from London on 17 September 1921 amidst a blaze of publicity. The ship proved a problem from the start and Shackleton had to change his plans several times en route south to accommodate delays caused by the need to work on its engines. By the time the *Quest* reached Rio at the end of November, he was in poor spirits. His aims for the expedition seemed uncertain. 'The Boss says,' one man confided to his diary, 'quite frankly that he does not know what he will do.' The plan, such as it was, appeared to be to head for the Antarctic islands and review the possibilities there. The truth was that Shackleton was ill. He died of a heart attack in South Georgia, aged only forty-seven, on 5 January 1922. Plans were made to return his body to Britain but a message was received from his wife, saying that he should be buried on South Georgia. The grave of the man who was indisputably one of the great figures of the Heroic Age of polar exploration now stands in the cemetery at Grytviken where it is regularly visited by tourists on the cruise ships that now sail Antarctic waters.

Wings Over the South: Byrd, Ellsworth and Others

With Shackleton dead and other explorers more interested in the North, the exploration of Antarctica was briefly left, as it had been a century earlier, to whalers and sealers. The most important of these was Lars Christensen, a wealthy Norwegian ship-owner and whaling magnate who sailed on a number of expeditions southwards and sponsored several others.

In the Arctic the years between 1925 and 1928 had been marked by a swift succession of expeditions and enterprises. As the 1920s drew to a close, this frenetic activity was replicated in the South. Many of the same men who had competed in the northern latitudes now turned their attention to the Antarctic. Hubert Wilkins, knighted after his trans-Arctic feats, was financed by the American press baron William Randolph Hearst (supposedly the model for Orson Welles's Citizen Kane) to fly over Antarctica. Richard Byrd who had entered what he later called 'the hero business' through his exploits in the North now looked to burnish his heroic reputation with the American people by travelling to the opposite end of the earth. As Byrd wrote in 1928, 'Aviation cannot claim mastery of the globe until the South Pole and its vast surrounding mystery be opened up by airplane.'

He and his rivals now intended to do exactly that. The media eagerly promoted what was seen as a new race for the South Pole, this time conducted in the air.

On 20 December 1928, Wilkins, together with Carl Ben Eielson, the pilot who had shared his Arctic adventure, took off on what was the first significant aircraft flight in Antarctic history (Eielson had taken his plane up a month earlier but only for twenty minutes) and flew over territory that no one else had ever seen. The trip was not as ambitious as Wilkins had originally hoped. He had problems getting enough fuel on board to take him anything like as far as he had planned. However, as he noted in his diary, 'For the first time in history, new land was being discovered from the air.' Word of the flight soon reached Richard Byrd at his new base on the Ross Sea, not far from Amundsen's Framheim. Byrd had arrived there at the end of 1928 in command of the largest, best-equipped and most lavishly funded expedition so far sent to Antarctica and established what he called Little America, a substantial conglomeration of huts for his men and hangars for his aircraft. Together with a pilot Bernt Balchen, co-pilot and radio operator Harold June and a cameraman named Ashley McKinley to record his achievements, Byrd set off on 28 November 1929, nearly a year after Wilkins had made his pioneering flight. In less than nineteen hours they were at Little America again, having flown to the pole and back. What had cost Scott and his men months of back-breaking labour and eventually their lives, Byrd had achieved in a day. He had not actually landed at the pole, judging that there was no chance of rescue if the plane could not get back into the air, but he had shown just what aircraft in the Antarctic could do. And, thanks to radio signals sent by Harold June, news of the flight was transmitted back to the USA even before it was over.

Byrd returned to the Antarctic in another expedition between 1933 and 1935, by which time he had another rival amidst the ice. Lincoln Ellsworth, who had backed Amundsen's last expeditions, had turned his attention south. Sailing on a ship which he named *Wyatt Earp* after one of his heroes, Ellsworth arrived at the Bay of Whales, close to Byrd's Little America base, in January 1934. With him were Hubert Wilkins, who had hitched his star to that of the wealthy American, and the pilot Bernt Balchen whose job was to assist Ellsworth in the achievement of his ambitious goal – a Transantarctic flight. A first attempt that year failed when the plane they planned to use was badly damaged in the ice and Ellsworth returned to the USA. He was soon back and a second attempt was undertaken. This was to fly across the continent in the other direction and end up at Little America, rather than starting from there, but it too met with difficulties. A third attempt was planned for 1935 but a new pilot was needed. Bernt Balchen had had enough. In his place, Ellsworth recruited a Canadian named Herbert Hollick-Kenyon who had been a member of the Royal Flying Corps during the First World War. On 23 November, the two men set off from an island at the north-eastern tip of the Antarctic Peninsula and headed across the Antarctic continent. After travelling some 2200 miles, much of it over unmapped territory which Ellsworth airily claimed for the USA, and discovering the highest mountain range in Antarctica which he named after himself, they finally made it to Little America where they were holed up, out of radio contact with the rest of the world, for a month before being picked up by a British research ship that was sailing in the Bay of Whales. Ellsworth returned to the Antarctic for one more expedition at the end of the 1930s but nothing could quite match the achievement of the first Transantarctic flight

At much the same time as Byrd and others were instigating a new era in Antarctic exploration, a veteran of the Heroic Age returned to the continent when Douglas Mawson led the British Australian and New Zealand Antarctic Research Expedition. Sailing on Captain Scott's old ship, the *Discovery*, Mawson and his team of scientists carried out significant work in a variety of disciplines from geology (Mawson's own field) to oceanography but there was also an unmistakeable sense that the expedition was there to plant flags and claim territory. Mapping of territory was linked with proclamations of sovereignty over the new land that was being mapped. What was later to be known as the Australian Antarctic Territory was in the process of being charted and defined.

The BANZARE was one of the very few ventures southwards by British or Commonwealth expeditions during the inter-war years. Since the death of Shackleton, public enthusiasm for such projects had waned and the government was unwilling to put money behind them. The only other enterprise of any note in the 1920s and 1930s was the British Graham Land expedition which left for Antarctica in 1934. Led by the Australian-born John Rymill, who had been on both of Gino Watkins's expeditions to Greenland, it was mostly privately financed, although the Colonial Office had made a small contribution to the funds. During the three years that Rymill and the men with him were away, they charted coastline that had not previously been mapped and proved that Graham Land, hitherto thought by many Antarctic experts to be an archipelago with a channel running through it that connected the Ross and Weddell Seas, was in fact a peninsula. The British government might no longer be enthusiastic about polar exploration but it was clear that there was still much to discover in Antarctica, even about its basic geography.

However, if Britain was drawing back from Antarctic exploration, other nations were showing interest in the continent. Nazi Germany had already revealed a fascination with the wilder shores of archaeological and geographical discovery. Expeditions had been despatched by Heinrich Himmler's pseudo-scientific institute, the Ahnenerbe, to Scandinavia and Central Europe. One to Tibet was long planned. Now it was the turn of Antarctica. Led by Alfred Ritscher, a sixty-year-old naval captain who had had some experience in Arctic waters as a young man, an expedition left Hamburg on 17 December 1938. Its aim, in Ritscher's words, was 'to secure for Germany her share in the approaching division of the Antarctic among the world powers'. In pursuit of that aim, his ship the *Schwabenland* arrived in an area of the continent which had already been claimed by Norway as Queen Maud Land. Ignoring any Norwegian claims, Ritscher's men landed on what they now decided was called Neu-Schwabenland and cheerfully began to plant Nazi flags amidst the ice and snow. They then made a series of airplane flights inland, scattering swastikas on the ground beneath them, before returning to Germany in April 1939. Any potential disputes with Norway over Queen Maud Land/Neu-Schwabenland which might have arisen were soon forgotten later in the year as events in the wider world overtook them.

Post-War: Power Politics in the South and Fuchs Crosses the Antarctic

For much of the war years, Antarctica was unvisited. In a time of world war, as had been shown between 1914 and 1918, there was little immediate incentive for exploration. Richard Byrd led his third expedition south in 1939 and remained in Antarctica until 1941, by which time it was growing more likely that the USA would soon be entering the war. The bases that Byrd had established were closed and their staff evacuated. In January 1944, Lieutenant James Marr who, as a Boy Scout, had travelled on Shackleton's last expedition, set off from the Falklands in what was dubbed Operation Tabarin. He established three bases in different parts of Antarctica which became the first permanent bases on the continent. Partly this may have been a response to German naval activity in the polar seas (vessels were sheltering in harbours in Antarctic islands and emerging to attack Allied shipping) but it was mainly an attempt to assert territorial rights against potential incursions from South American countries such as Chile and Argentina.

Many of the expeditions in the 1920s and 1930s had been

complicated by questions of territorial claims and sovereignty. Who owned these vast areas of icy wilderness? How was a claim to territory to be legally staked? Which nations had territorial rights to which regions of Antarctica? Explorers such as Byrd and Wilkins, Mawson and Christensen had not only been mapping tens of thousands of square miles of undiscovered land. They had, either implicitly or explicitly, been laying claim to them for their respective nations. There were now parts of the continent that were seen as 'belonging' in some way to Australia or Britain, to America or Norway. The process only became more complicated after the war.

The Americans, unsurprisingly, became increasingly active in these immediate post-war years. Expeditions were despatched south which dwarfed those of earlier days in manpower, resources and ambition. Richard Byrd, although now in his late fifties, was involved with most of them. His name and reputation added prestige to any expedition which could claim them. Operation High Jump in 1946–47 involved thirteen ships, many more aircraft and thousands of men and resulted in the establishment of a large base, the fourth to be given the name Little America. This was followed the next year by the almost equally ambitious Operation Windmill. Meanwhile, in January 1947, the Ronne Antarctic Research Expedition, named after its leader, set sail from Texas. Finn Ronne was born in Norway in 1899, the son of a man who had been with Amundsen on his South Pole expedition, but had emigrated to the US as a young man. He had served in two of Byrd's 1930s expeditions and now took charge of what was the last major, privately sponsored American expedition to Antarctica. It mapped vast areas of the continent that remained uncharted, mostly from the air, and the last significant stretches of the coastline that remained unexplored. It also proved conclusively what had long been suspected and what Rymill had more or less demonstrated in the 30s – that there was no connecting channel between the Ross Sea and the Weddell Sea. American activities in Antarctica in the decade or so after the war culminated in Operation Deep Freeze, a series of interconnected missions in the years 1955 and 1956, again under the overall aegis of Richard Byrd. The name has since come to be applied to US operations in the Antarctic right up to the present day.

Cold War rivalries were now being played out in the Far South. By this time, the Soviets were showing signs of rediscovering a Russian interest in the Antarctic which had been dormant for well over a century. Bellingshausen's pioneering voyage of 1820 was re-examined and claims of precedence based on it were advanced. Russian whaling ships began to visit Antarctic waters in 1947 but, in 1955, the first, state-sponsored Soviet expedition, under the leadership of oceanographer Mikhail Somov, arrived on the continent. Its main task was the establishment of Mirny, a permanent science station on the coast of the Davis Sea which took its name (meaning 'peaceful') from that of one of the support ships used in Bellingshausen's expedition. Two further Soviet expeditions followed in swift succession to coincide with International Geophysical Year, a worldwide series of ambitious projects in the earth sciences in 1957–58. More research stations were established on the Antarctic continent.

In the complicated post-war era, with its Cold War tensions and sovereignty disputes, it seemed impossible to return to the simpler heroism of an earlier age but, if any expedition could claim such status it was the Commonwealth Trans-Antarctic Expedition, led by the Englishman Vivian Fuchs. Supported by the British, Australian and New Zealand governments, it had, of course, its political dimensions but it was possible to present it as an old-fashioned adventure and the media did exactly that. Its stature as such was only enhanced by the announcement that Edmund Hillary, the mountaineer who had recently been one of the first two men to stand on the summit of Mount Everest, was to be part of it and would lead the support group that approached the pole from the Ross Sea. In November 1957, Fuchs and his men left Shackleton Base on the Weddell Sea and headed south. From Scott Base on the Ross Sea, Hillary made his way in a similar direction. The two parties met at the South Pole, the first men to reach the pole overland since Scott and Amundsen, and then they all travelled to Scott Base. The first overland crossing of the continent had been successfully completed.

However it was presented in the press, the Commonwealth Trans-Antarctic Expedition could not disguise the fact that Antarctica was now the site of tension and potential dispute between the nations that laid claim to territory within it. International law needed to be applied there. In June 1961, the Antarctic Treaty came into force. The original signatories, all of whom had long-standing interests and claims in the continent, were Argentina, Australia, Belgium, Britain, Chile, France, Japan, New Zealand, Norway, South Africa, the Soviet Union and the USA. By far the most significant of its articles were those which guaranteed freedom of scientific research in Antarctica and banned military activity there. In the half-century since its inception, other nations have signed the treaty and further agreements have been made which have extended or revised its provisions but the fundamental rules of international interaction on the continent established in 1961 are still in place.

The Poles in the Last Fifty Years

By the end of the 1950s, the task of exploring both the Arctic and the Antarctic was, in effect, accomplished. There were no more blank spaces on the maps. The lands surrounding both the North Pole and the South Pole had been fully charted. This did not mean, however, that people no longer had any incentive to visit them. Both the Arctic territories and Antarctica have seen more visitors by far in the last few decades than they have had in the previous two centuries. In Antarctica, at any given time, there are thousands of men and women in a continent that until recently was populated only by penguins and seals. Most of these are the scientists working at the array of permanent bases that have been established across the Antarctic mainland.

In both the North and the South, but particularly in the Arctic, the individual adventurer still found opportunities to mount expeditions. In 1968, the Englishman Wally Herbert, who had spent much of the 1950s in surveying work in Antarctica, turned his attention to the other end of the earth and organised a journey of some 3,500 miles on foot from Alaska to Spitsbergen via the North Pole. Ranulph Fiennes is probably the best-known adventurer of recent decades. Together with Charles Burton, he took part in the Transglobe Expedition between 1979 and 1982 and they became the first men to travel on the earth's surface to both its poles.

Gdansk-born Marek Kaminski entered the record books by doing the same feat in 1995 but solo. He pre-empted any possible jokes at his expense by calling his second expedition of the year 'A Pole at the Poles'. The first women at the South Pole were a group which arrived by plane in 1969. Twenty years later the Americans Victoria Murden and Shirley Metz became the first women to get there on foot. The first woman to travel to the North Pole on foot was Ann Bancroft, a member of the Will Steger International Polar Expedition, in 1986. She has been followed by many other intrepid women pioneers.

The polar regions have now become more than just destinations for those exceptionally brave individuals who are prepared to undergo extreme tests of physical endurance. Thanks to the huge improvements in technology, safety and methods of transport, it is now possible to visit both the Arctic and the Antarctic as a tourist. The numbers of passengers on cruise ships visiting Antarctica have actually fallen in recent years but, between November 2011 and April 2012, there were still nearly 30,000 people who were prepared to make the journey. As cruise ships sail through the ice in the south and dozens of companies offer adventure holidays beyond the Arctic Circle, it's all a far cry from Scott trapped in his tent on his doomed journey back from the pole or Franklin and his men disappearing into the Arctic wilderness, their final fate never to be fully explained. Without the exploits of the polar explorers – some successful, many catastrophic failures – the map of the world would still be covered with blank spaces at its north and south. Whatever their shortcomings, the best of them added to the sum of human knowledge about the earth on which we live.

The Polar Regions in the Imagination

The Polar Regions in Literature: From Frankenstein to Beryl Bainbridge

For the last two centuries and more, the polar regions have not been just geographical areas awaiting discovery by intrepid explorers; they have also been spaces in which poets and novelists have allowed their imaginations to travel. In Mary Shelley's *Frankenstein*, first published in 1818, the very year that Ross's first expedition in search of the Northwest Passage departed, the North Pole is a place of emptiness and desolation to which the Monster departs to face its death. Twenty years earlier, the southern ocean had been the setting in which Coleridge's Ancient Mariner brings a curse upon himself when he kills the albatross. Since that era, many other writers have found inspiration in the white spaces of the world.

The Franklin expedition, with its story of suffering and endurance and the continuing questions marks over the exact fate of the men of the *Erebus* and *Terror*, stirred the imaginations of many writers in the Victorian era. As we have seen, Dickens was fascinated by it and, although he did not feature it in his fiction, he published a long article 'The Lost Arctic Voyagers' in his magazine *Household Words*. He was also the prime mover behind the staging of a play by his close friend Wilkie Collins which very obviously draws upon the Franklin expedition for its plot. *The Frozen Deep*, a story of heroic self-sacrifice during a voyage in search of the Northwest Passage, was given a number of well-publicised amateur performances in the 1850s, including one attended by Queen Victoria. Dickens not only rewrote parts of the play and encouraged Collins to re-jig its plot to emphasise the heroism of its central character Richard Wardour, he also played Wardour himself. The central character in Jules Verne's *The Adventures of Captain Hatteras*, the leader of a British expedition to the North Pole, carries echoes of Sir John Franklin.

Nor is the Franklin expedition an exclusively nineteenth-century obsession. It has been the subject of a surprising number of modern novels. In *The Broken Lands*, first published in 1992, Robert Edric avoids indulging in the twenty-twenty vision of historical hindsight. He doesn't delight in exposing feet of clay or highlight hypocrisies with a knowing irony. The heroism of Franklin and his men, although seen from a perspective unavailable to the explorer's contemporaries, is not radically undermined. Instead we see men gradually destroyed by their own, necessarily, blinkered assumptions about the world and by an unforgiving natural environment in which the moral values of the society from which they come cannot save them. The ice which traps them and the landscape in which they make their harrowing and ultimately futile journey back towards civilisation are brilliantly evoked in a book which follows, with convincing psychological realism, their inexorable decline. The German novelist Sten Nadolny's *The Discovery of Slowness*, published in the previous decade, is a strange but satisfying reconstruction of Franklin's life and the explorer features in William Vollman's epic novel *The Rifles*. Rudy Wiebe's prize-winning Canadian novel *A Discovery of Strangers* focuses on one of Franklin's expeditions from the 1820s. There is even a contemporary horror novel by Dan Simmons (*The Terror*) in which Franklin and his men are stalked across the Arctic ice by a monster drawn from Inuit mythology.

Other novelists have drawn on the Franklin search expeditions to create their fiction. One of the central characters in Andrea Barrett's *The Voyage of the Narwhal* owes a lot to real explorers like Elisha Kent Kane. Steven Heighton's *Afterlands* is the story of another imaginary expedition, this one from the 1870s, which echoes those that really took place.

In *The Terrors of Ice and Darkness*, Christoph Ransmayr cleverly weaves together two stories – one of the Austro-Hungarian North Pole expedition of 1872–74 and the other of a contemporary Italian whose obsession with it takes him north – to create a fascinating and unsettling novel. Wayne Johnston's *The Navigator of New York* is a Canadian novel which focuses on Robert Peary and Frederick Cook and the controversies surrounding their conflicting claims to be first at the North Pole. And, of course, there have long been thrillers set in the Arctic, of which Alistair MacLean's *Ice Station Zebra*, first published in 1963, still remains one of the most famous.

Like the Arctic, Antarctica has proved to be a vast white space on which writers have been able to project their imaginings. Edgar Allan Poe was one of the first to do so. In his only completed novel, *The Narrative of Arthur Gordon Pym of Nantucket*, the eponymous hero is driven ever further south, through shipwreck, mutiny and encounters with the black natives of a polar land, towards a mystical encounter at the South Pole with which the book abruptly ends. Other writers, most of them influenced by Poe, found their imaginations as stirred as his by thoughts of the bleak wonders and potential mysteries to be encountered in the Far South. Verne's *An Antarctic Mystery* (1897) is explicitly a sequel to Poe's work. William Clark Russell, largely forgotten today, was a well-known writer of maritime fiction in Victorian England. (Sherlock Holmes's companion, Dr Watson, is reading a novel by Russell at the beginning of one of Conan Doyle's short stories about the great detective.) Russell's book *The Frozen Pirate* (1887) is the story of a shipwrecked American sailor who drifts ever further south on an iceberg and eventually comes across a pirate ship frozen in the ice many years earlier. Another forgotten writer,

James De Mille, imagined a lush southern land populated by extinct creatures in *A Strange Manuscript Found in a Copper Cylinder* published in 1888 and, in the 1890s, Antarctica became a favourite location for writers of the 'lost world' fiction that was popular at the time.

Poe is an obvious influence on HP Lovecraft but the horror writer of the 1920s and 1930s was equally clearly thinking of Richard Byrd's flights across the Antarctic continent when he produced *At the Mountains of Madness*. Originally written in 1931, when Byrd was front-page news, although not published until 1936, Lovecraft's novella recounts the story of an expedition to Antarctica which stumbles across the relics of an alien civilisation so appalling and unearthly that members of the expedition are driven mad by what they see of it. Lovecraft was not alone in his fascination with the Far South. The pages of American pulp magazines of the thirties and forties are filled with stories in which Antarctica is populated with everything from lost Neanderthals to the survivors of Atlantis. Apart from *At the Mountains of Madness*, probably the best of these is John W Campbell's classic novella *Who Goes There?* which first appeared in *Astounding Stories* in 1938. The basis for John Carpenter's film *The Thing*, the story is set on a remote research station in Antarctica.

In science fiction, the interest in the region has continued to the present day, although the narratives have certainly grown more sophisticated. Kim Stanley Robinson's *Antarctica*, for example, is a thriller about the threats to the continent in a near future where environmentalists and multinational companies have very different views about its potential.

Just as writers in recent years have been fascinated by Franklin and his fellow Arctic voyagers, so others have found inspiration in the great stories of Antarctic exploration. Thomas Keneally has twice written novels in which the central character is a man looking back on his experiences in the Antarctic many years earlier. In *The Survivor* the protagonist remembers a disastrous expedition in which the leader lost his life; *Victim of the Aurora* is a clever murder mystery set against the backdrop of a fictional expedition in 1909, as recollected by one of the participants. One of the late Beryl Bainbridge's finest novels is *The Birthday Boys*, which looks at Scott's last expedition from the perspectives of several of those involved in it and the *Terra Nova* expedition is also the subject of a very different novel – Robert Ryan's *Death on the Ice*. *The Ice-Cold Heaven* by the German novelist Mirko Bonné provides an account of Shackleton's *Endurance* expedition as seen by the real-life teenage stowaway Perce Blackborow, cunningly disguised in the novel as Merce Blackboro.

The Polar Regions in the Visual Arts

Some of the most telling and evocative images of the Arctic and the Antarctic were created by those who travelled to the polar regions themselves. In the nineteenth century, many naval officers, particularly those trained as cartographers, were skilled as draughtsmen and watercolour painters and some of those who travelled to the Far South and the Far North recorded what they saw. George Back was particularly gifted as an artist. Others who painted or drew what they had seen with particular success included Samuel Gurney Cresswell, who served in the Arctic under James Clark Ross and Robert McClure, and a midshipman with the appropriate name of Horatio Nelson Head whose sketch of the two ships on Parry's third voyage dwarfed by towering cliffs of ice is one of the most evocative Arctic images of the whole nineteenth century.

Professional artists too began to respond to what they had heard or read of the Arctic. The German romantic painter Caspar David Friedrich produced *Das Eismeer* ('The Sea of Ice') in the 1820s. The Arctic became a regular motif in the paintings of a wide range of nineteenth-century painters. *The Icebergs* by the American painter Frederic Church, like the vistas of Niagara Falls for which he was already famous, was originally intended to be a scene of sublime nature untouched by human presence. When it was displayed in London in 1863, he painted in the broken mast of a ship, a hint of sailors lost like Franklin's men in the icy wastes. The following year, one of Victoria's favourite painters, Edwin Landseer, exhibited *Man Proposes, God Disposes*, a canvas on which one polar bear tears at the sails of a wrecked ship while another has the rib of a skeletal mariner in its mouth. The reference to the Franklin expedition is clear. Other great names in Victorian art were also drawn to the subject

John Millais's *The North-West Passage*, painted in 1874 just before the Nares expedition sailed, made only oblique reference to Franklin and those others who had been lost in the Arctic in its depiction of a grizzled seafarer, at home with his daughter, but clearly daydreaming (or having waking nightmares) of his past experiences amidst the ice. At least one well-known painter – the American William Bradford – became a traveller in the Far North himself, making several trips to Labrador and Greenland in the 1860s and bringing back material to help him in the creation of his Arctic landscapes. On one of them, he was accompanied by Isaac Israel Hayes who had his own terrifying memories of the ice and snow from previous journeys.

As the nineteenth century went on, photography became increasingly more sophisticated in both its artistry and its technology and the expeditions of the Heroic Age of Antarctic Exploration nearly all employed an official photographer. Herbert Ponting, already well-known as a photographer producing images of exotic places for London magazines, travelled on Scott's *Terra Nova* expedition; Frank Hurley was an Australian who accompanied both Mawson and Shackleton on expeditions. Both produced some of the most iconic images of the Antarctic ever committed to film. The Heroic Age also coincided with the beginnings of documentary film-making and images of men struggling against the elements in icy landscapes made stirring viewing for stay-at-home audiences. Hurley took a movie camera with him on Mawson's expedition of 1911–14 and on Shackleton's ill-fated *Endurance* expedition. His films *Home of the Blizzard* (1913) and *South* (1919) emerged from the footage he shot. They were the first in a succession of distinguished documentaries which, over the decades, brought the polar wilderness before the eyes of cinema audiences around the world. *The Great White Silence* of 1924 made use of footage and photographs shot by Ponting on the *Terra Nova* expedition. It was not a great success on its first release but it was restored and re-released as recently as 2011 to much acclaim and enthusiasm. In the sound era, Ponting produced *Ninety Degrees South* (1933) which thrilled those who saw it. *With Byrd at the South Pole* came out in 1930, advertised in breathless, almost disbelieving tones as 'Actually filmed in the vast unknown of the Antarctic', and won an Academy Award for best cinematography.

Fictional films about the polar regions began to appear in the 1930s. Frank Capra's *Dirigible* from 1931 stars Fay Wray, later to be the subject of King Kong's infatuation, in a story of pilots competing to reach the South Pole and (incidentally) for the love of Miss Wray's character. 1933 saw an American/German co-production entitled *SOS Iceberg/SOS Eisberg*, an example of cinematic co-operation that was to be rapidly brought to a halt by the rise of the Nazis. (Ironically, one of the film's German stars, Leni Riefenstahl, was to become Hitler's favourite movie director.) Footage from it was later used in a Universal B-movie entitled *Mutiny in the Arctic*. There were even polar cartoons. Walt Disney Studios produced an early but inventive Silly Symphony entitled *Arctic Antics* (1930) which has polar bears, walruses and some badly-lost penguins dancing across ice floes and snow-covered landscapes. Ideas about the North and the South Pole, even if some of them were wrong ones, were now firmly embedded in popular culture.

In Britain, *Scott of the Antarctic*, produced at Ealing in 1948, stuck very firmly to the heroic narrative that had been established in the previous thirty-six years. It was only in 1985 that a revisionist version of the story, written by the left-wing playwright Trevor Griffiths and based on Roland Huntford's *Scott and Amundsen*, was produced. The seven-part TV drama *The Last Place on Earth*, starring Martin Shaw as Scott and Sverre Anker Ousdal as Amundsen, was as scathing in its portrayal of Scott as the biography on which it was based. *The Red Tent*, with Peter Finch as Umberto Nobile and Sean Connery as Amundsen, was an international co-production from 1969 which told its own version, not always historically accurate, of the polar journey of the airship *Italia* and its crash.

In recent cinema and television, virtually every genre of movie has its examples of polar stories. There are documentaries by the dozen but there are also feature-length cartoons (*Happy Feet* and its sequel), thrillers (*The Last Winter*), TV science fiction series and children's films. And, of course, there are horror movies. By the 1950s, both the Arctic and the Antarctic were amongst the most popular places from which monsters emerged in schlock films such as *The Beast from 20,000 Fathoms* and the trend has continued to the present day. From vampires enjoying the long periods of darkness (*30 Days of Night*) to Nazi zombies (the Norwegian film *Dead Snow*), strange and terrifying creatures emerge out of the white wildernesses that we still do not feel we fully understand.

Polar Explorers:
A Brief Biographical Dictionary

Luigi Amedeo, Duke of the Abruzzi (1873–1933)
A grandson of the Italian king, Victor Emmanuel II, and the son of a man who was briefly King of Spain, the Duke of the Abruzzi (as he was usually known) was a member of the highest levels of European aristocracy. He was also an adventurer who travelled the world in order to satisfy his passion for mountaineering. In 1899–1900, he led a failed expedition to the North Pole.

Jameson Adams (1880–1962)
With experience in both the Merchant Navy and the Royal Navy, Adams joined Shackleton's *Nimrod* expedition as its second in command in 1907. He was one of the four men who reached a Furthest South of 88° 23′ in January 1909.

Roald Amundsen (1872–1928)
Amundsen is a towering figure in polar history and some historians even argue that he was the first man to reach the North Pole as well as the first to make it to the South Pole. Born in Norway, he was a member of de Gerlache's *Belgica* expedition to the Antarctic in 1897–99. On board a small ship named the *Gjoa*, he was the leader of the first expedition to traverse the Northwest Passage in 1903–06. While planning an attempt on the North Pole in 1909, he heard about Peary's claims to have got there and changed his plans. He travelled south instead and journeyed with four other men to the South Pole, beating Scott

to the goal by a matter of weeks. In 1926, he flew in the airship *Norge* to the North Pole, accompanied by Lincoln Ellsworth and Umberto Nobile. He lost his life two years later while searching for Nobile who had disappeared on another polar trip.

Salomon August Andrée (1854–1897)

Andrée was a Swedish engineer with an interest in aeronautics who was convinced that the best way to reach the North Pole was to travel there by balloon. In 1897, with two companions, he set off in his balloon, *The Eagle*, to prove his case. He was never seen alive again. It was not until 1930 that the fate of the expedition was discovered.

George Back (1796–1878)

Born in Stockport, Back joined the navy as a boy. He served as a young officer in Franklin's disastrous first voyage in the Arctic and in the same commander's more successful second one. In the 1830s he commanded two expeditions himself. On the first he became the first white man to see the large river in northern Canada which is named after him; on the second, he nearly lost his ship after it was icebound north of Hudson Bay for many months.

William Baffin (c.1584–1622)

Baffin's early life is largely a mystery but it is known that he sailed on an expedition to Greenland in 1612. He returned to the Arctic three years later and then, in 1616, he sailed further north than anyone else had done at the time and discovered the bay that now bears his name. He later joined the East India Company and was killed in an attack on a Portuguese garrison in the Persian Gulf.

Willem Barents (c.1550–1597)

Born in the Frisian Islands off the Dutch coast, Barents was one of the earliest explorers to search for a Northeast Passage from the Atlantic to the Pacific. In the 1590s, he undertook three voyages in the seas north of the Siberian coast. On the last of these he made the first sighting of Spitsbergen but his ship was caught in the winter ice. He died during a boat journey towards safety and was buried on an island in the Novaya Zemlya archipelago.

Robert Bartlett (1875–1946)
Born in Newfoundland, Bartlett became one of the most experienced Arctic travellers of the first half of the twentieth century. He accompanied Peary on three expeditions and was desperately disappointed not to be included in the party that headed for the pole in 1909. During Stefansson's disastrous *Karluk* expedition in 1914, it was Bartlett who made a heroic march across the ice to bring help when the ship sank. He also captained the ship which took Richard Byrd to the Arctic for his flight to the North Pole in 1926.

Frederick Beechey (1796–1856)
The son of a well-known portrait painter, Beechey was a naval officer who first went to the Arctic with Franklin in 1818. He returned there twice on other expeditions in the 1820s. Beechey Island is named after him.

Edward Belcher (1799–1877)
Belcher had travelled with Beechey to the Bering Strait and was later to make the first survey of Hong Kong after it came into British hands in 1841. In 1852, he was in overall command of several ships that formed the last government-sponsored expedition to search for Sir John Franklin and his men.

Fabian von Bellingshausen (1778–1852)
A naval officer born in what is now Estonia, Bellingshausen played a major role in the first Russian circumnavigation of the world in the first years of the nineteenth century. Between 1819

and 1821, he was the commander of the Russian expedition which first sighted the Antarctic continent and sailed around it.

John Biscoe (1794–1843)

After serving in the Royal Navy in the Anglo-American War of 1812–15, Biscoe became a captain on merchant ships and was chosen by the whaling company Enderby & Sons to lead an expedition in search of new hunting grounds in 1830. While becoming the third man in history to circumnavigate the Antarctic continent, he made several significant sightings of land which he named after his patron and the First Lord of the Admiralty at the time.

Olav Bjaaland (1873–1961)

An expert skier who had won numerous prizes in competitions in Norway and elsewhere, Bjaaland joined Amundsen's polar expedition in 1910 and was one of the five men to reach the South Pole in December 1911.

Carsten Borchgrevink (1864–1934)

The Anglo-Norwegian Borchgrevink made his first voyage to Antarctica on a whaling ship captained by Henrik Bull in 1894–95. Several years later, he was the leader of the Southern Cross Expedition, the first to spend a winter on the Antarctic continent.

Henry Bowers (1883–1912)

Known to everyone as 'Birdie' because of the beak-like prominence of his nose, Bowers was a young officer in the Royal Indian Marine Service who joined Scott's *Terra Nova* expedition. He accompanied Wilson and Cherry-Garrard on the so-called 'worst journey in the world' in the winter of July 1911 and was chosen by Scott to be one of the final polar party five months later. He died in the tent with his leader on the way back from the pole.

Edward Bransfield (1785–1852)

An Irish officer in the Royal Navy, Bransfield was stationed in South America when he was despatched southwards to investigate talk of islands recently discovered beyond Cape Horn. In January 1820, he was one of the first navigators to sight the Antarctic continent.

William S Bruce (1867–1921)

Born in London into a Scottish family, Bruce studied at the University of Edinburgh and made his first trip to Antarctica on a whaling ship in 1892. After several voyages to the Arctic later in the decade, he led the Scottish National Antarctic Expedition between 1902 and 1904. Later plans for a transcontinental Antarctic expedition had to be abandoned for lack of funding.

Richard E Byrd (1888–1957)

A member of a wealthy and politically powerful family from Virginia, Byrd was a pioneering American aviator who undertook a series of significant flights over both the Arctic and the Antarctic and organised major expeditions to the Far North and the Far South. In 1926, he undertook a controversial flight which, he claimed, took him to the North Pole. Two years later he led his first expedition to the Antarctic and flew to the South Pole in November 1929. He organised four more expeditions to the continent and became America's most famous Antarctic explorer.

Umberto Cagni (1863–1932)

A mountaineering companion of the Duke of the Abruzzi, Cagni journeyed to the Arctic with his friend in 1899. When the Duke lost toes to frostbite and was unable to lead the trip towards the pole, Cagni took over command. He reached a new Farthest North but failed to get as far as the pole.

Jean-Baptiste Charcot (1867–1936)

The son of a famous neurologist, Charcot became a doctor himself but his passion was for the sea and exploration. He was the leader of two French expeditions to Antarctica, in 1904–07 and 1908–10, both of which charted long stretches of Antarctic coastline for the first time.

Apsley Cherry-Garrard (1886–1959)

As a young man, Cherry-Garrard was a member of the *Terra Nova* expedition and was one of the party which discovered the bodies of Scott, Wilson and Bowers in November 1912. With Bowers and Wilson he had earlier travelled to Cape Crozier in search of penguin eggs in the winter of 1911, an epic trip he described in his classic account of polar exploration, *The Worst Journey in the World*.

Richard Collinson (1811–1883)

One of the many naval officers employed in the long search for the Franklin expedition, Collinson captained HMS *Enterprise* when it entered the Arctic Ocean from the Bering Strait in 1851. He found no trace of Franklin but spent two winters amidst the ice.

Frederick A Cook (1865–1940)

Cook's first trip to the Arctic was on an expedition led by Robert Peary in the early 1890s. He was the doctor on de Gerlache's *Belgica* expedition to the Antarctic in 1897–99. He led two expeditions to Mount McKinley between 1903 and 1906, on the second of which he said he had reached the summit. His claim was later proved to be false. His claim that he reached the North Pole in April 1908 was also shown to owe more to imagination than reality.

James Cook (1728–1779)

The greatest navigator of his age (arguably of all time), Cook made significant contributions to the history of both the Arctic and the Antarctic. On his second voyage, in January 1773, his ships became the first to cross the Antarctic Circle and, although he never sighted the Antarctic mainland, his extensive travels in the southern oceans proved that *Terra Australis*, a temperate and well-populated land long thought to exist there, was nothing more than a fable. On his third voyage, which culminated in his death on a Hawaiian beach, Cook sailed up the west coast of America and Canada, looking for an entrance into a Northwest Passage but was unable to find one.

Tom Crean (1877–1938)

Crean was an Irish seaman who was a member of several of the most important Antarctic expeditions of the Edwardian era. He joined Scott's *Discovery* expedition after another man deserted in New Zealand and so impressed his leader that he was invited to travel south with the *Terra Nova* in 1910. He also served on Shackleton's *Endurance* expedition and was one of the men who travelled with him on the rescue mission from Elephant Island to South Georgia.

Francis Crozier (1796–c.1848)

Born in Ireland, Crozier was a British naval officer who took part in half a dozen polar expeditions from the 1820s to the 1840s. He was a close friend of James Clark Ross and was second in command during Ross's four-year voyage in Antarctic waters. He held the same position in John Franklin's ill-fated final expedition and took command after Franklin's death. He is assumed to have died with the rest of the men some time during their failed attempts to walk to safety after their ships were trapped in the ice.

Edgeworth David (1858–1934)

David was a Welsh-born geologist who spent most of his working life in Australia. In 1907 he joined Shackleton's *Nimrod* expedition to Antarctica. Although he was nearly fifty, David led two of the most successful journeys of the expedition – the ascent of Mount Erebus and the location of the South Magnetic Pole.

Edwin De Haven (1816–1865)

As a career officer in the US Navy, De Haven took part in the United States Exploring Expedition led by Charles Wilkes between 1839 and 1842. Because of his experience with the USEE, De Haven was chosen to command the first expedition sponsored by Henry Grinnell to look for Sir John Franklin in 1850–51. Although he visited Beechey Island soon after Ommanney had found evidence of Franklin's winter camp there, De Haven was able to report nothing new about the lost expedition and, after months trapped by the ice, was forced to return to the USA.

George W DeLong (1844–1881)

With the backing of the eccentric newspaper owner James G Bennett, DeLong sailed for the Arctic in the USS *Jeannette* in 1879, hoping to find a route to the North Pole. The voyage was a disaster. The *Jeannette* was trapped in the ice and DeLong and his men were forced to abandon it and take to its ship's boats. DeLong reached the shores of Siberia on one of the boats but perished there.

Erich von Drygalski (1865–1949)

Born in Königsberg in Prussia (now Kaliningrad in Russia), Drygalski was a scientist who led two German expeditions to the Arctic in the early 1890s. On board the ship the *Gauss*, he was in charge of an expedition to the Antarctic in 1901–03.

Jules Dumont D'Urville (1790–1842)

A scholarly French naval officer who had been instrumental in the discovery of the Venus de Milo, Dumont D'Urville led expeditions to the Pacific in the 1820s and to Antarctica in the

1830s. He discovered Adélie Land on the Antarctic continent and named it after his wife. Both he and she were killed in France's first major rail accident in 1842.

Lincoln Ellsworth (1880–1951)
The son of an extremely wealthy mine-owner and banker who was also interested in polar exploration, Ellsworth made his own contributions to discovery in both the Arctic and the Antarctic. He helped to fund Amundsen's flight over the North Pole in 1926 and accompanied the Norwegian explorer on the journey. He undertook a series of expeditions to Antarctica in the 1930s. The Ellsworth Mountains there are named after him.

Edgar Evans (1876–1912)
Evans, a Welsh seaman, impressed Captain Scott with his strength and powers of endurance on the *Discovery* expedition. He was invited to join Scott's second expedition on the *Terra Nova*. Although he had a reputation as a heavy drinker (he fell overboard while drunk when the *Terra Nova* was about to leave New Zealand), Scott had a high regard for him and took him in the final polar party. On the way back from the pole, Evans fell into a crevasse and suffered concussion, and he was the first of the group to die.

Edward Evans (1881–1957)
As a young naval officer, Evans served on the *Morning*, the ship which relieved Scott's *Discovery* expedition in 1903. He was planning his own journey to Antarctica when he was invited to become second in command of Scott's *Terra Nova* expedition. Evans had hopes of being in the final polar party in 1912 and was bitterly disappointed when he was told by Scott he was to turn back with the last support group. He nearly died on the return march and was invalided back to England. He went on to a distinguished naval career and ended his life as an admiral and 1st Baron Mountevans.

Ranulph Fiennes (b.1944)
Probably the best known of contemporary polar travellers, the impressively named Ranulph Twisleton-Wykeham-Fiennes is a former army officer who has led expeditions to many of the world's most remote areas, including both the Arctic and the Antarctic.

Wilhelm Filchner (1877–1957)
An adventurer who had travelled in Central Asia and Tibet as a young man, Filchner was chosen to lead a German Antarctic Expedition which left Germany in 1911. The original, ambitious plan for the expedition had been for a complete crossing of the Antarctic continent but Filchner, his ship caught in the ice of the Weddell Sea for long periods, had to content himself with making minor improvements to the mapping of the southern continent.

John Franklin (1786–1847)
Franklin was probably the most likeable and the least lucky of all the nineteenth-century explorers of the Arctic. His first expedition, along the Coppermine River and the coastline to its east, was a catastrophe more or less from the beginning and ended in near-starvation, murder and reports of cannibalism. He returned to the Arctic for a very much more successful expedition a few years later. After a period as governor of Van Diemen's Land, he was chosen in 1845 to lead the best-equipped expedition ever to look for the Northwest Passage. He and his ships entered the Arctic wilderness and were never heard from again, their disappearance initiating a series of searches which were unsuccessful in locating the missing men but added immeasurably to geographical knowledge of the region.

Martin Frobisher (c.1535–1594)
A Devon-born seafarer, Frobisher made three journeys in the 1570s in search of the Northwest Passage. He reached what is

now Baffin Island and discovered an ore which he believed (falsely) to be gold but he had no luck in finding any route to the Indies. He was knighted in 1588, not for his achievements as an explorer but for his role in the defeat of the Spanish Armada.

Vivian Fuchs (1908–1999)
Born in the Isle of Wight to a family of German extraction, Fuchs trained as a geologist at Cambridge and was a member of an expedition to the Arctic in 1929. After spending time in Africa and serving with distinction in the Second World War, he turned his attention to the Far South and involved himself in the work of the Falkland Islands Dependencies Survey. He was the leader of the Commonwealth Trans-Antarctic Expedition of 1955–58.

Adrien de Gerlache (1866–1934)
The Belgian de Gerlache led the first expedition that overwintered in Antarctica. On board the *Belgica*, he and his men (including Roald Amundsen and Frederick Cook) were trapped in the ice in February 1898 and obliged to spend a year, including several months in complete darkness, in trying to free themselves. De Gerlache later took the *Belgica* on several expeditions to Arctic waters but he never returned to the Far South.

Adolphus Greely (1844–1935)
A soldier and veteran of the American Civil War, Greely was given command of the so-called Lady Franklin Bay expedition which was to be the USA's contribution to the first International Polar Year in 1881. Although two members of the expedition achieved a new Farthest North of 83° 24', it ended in disaster, the deaths of most of the men and rumours of cannibalism.

Charles Francis Hall (1821–1871)
At one time a newspaper publisher in Cincinnati, Hall became obsessed by the Arctic long before he had ever travelled there.

He mounted three expeditions to the region between 1860 and his death. He died on the last of these, convinced that somebody else on the expedition had poisoned him – a possibility not entirely ruled out by examination of his body, exhumed a century after he had been buried in Greenland.

Helmer Hanssen (1870–1956)

After taking part in the successful traversing of the Northwest Passage in the ship *Gjoa*, Hanssen went with his captain on that voyage, Roald Amundsen, to Antarctica. He was one of the five men who reached the South Pole in December 1911. In 1919, he participated in Amundsen's *Maud* expedition.

Sverre Hassel (1876–1928)

A skilled and experienced dog driver, Hassel was one of the men with Amundsen when the Norwegian explorer reached the South Pole.

Isaac Israel Hayes (1832–1881)

A doctor from Pennsylvania, Hayes signed on as ship's surgeon to Kane's ill-fated expedition of 1853–55. In 1860, he led his own expedition to Ellesmere Island where he claimed to have sighted the Open Polar Sea. Hayes went on to serve in the American Civil War and became a politician in New York State.

Matthew Henson (1866–1955)

Born in Maryland, Henson had already had an adventurous career as a merchant seaman sailing around the world when he met Robert Peary in 1887 and was hired by him as a manservant. He accompanied Peary on all the older explorer's major expeditions and was with him on the journey which Peary claimed took them to the North Pole. Henson outlived his polar companion by more than thirty years and published his own account of their travels entitled *A Negro Explorer at the North Pole*.

Wally Herbert (1934–2007)

Probably the most successful polar traveller of the second half of the twentieth century, Herbert worked for the Falklands Islands Dependencies Survey in the 1950s and went on to retrace several of the routes of the great explorers of the Heroic Age of Antarctic Exploration. In 1968–69, he led the British Trans-Arctic Expedition, reaching the North Pole in April 1969. Because of doubts about previous journeys, Herbert's trek made him arguably the first man to reach the pole on foot.

Edmund Hillary (1919–2008)

Best known as one of the first two men to climb Everest in 1953, the New Zealand-born Edmund Hillary also took part in the Commonwealth Trans-Antarctic Expedition a few years later.

Henry Hudson (c.1560–c.1611)

The man who gave his name to Hudson Bay made a series of journeys to the Canadian Arctic between 1607 and his death. On the last of them he charted the coastline of his eponymous bay and, after wintering amidst the ice, wanted to head further north. His men were not so enthusiastic about the idea. They mutinied and set him, his son and a few loyal crew members adrift in an open boat. None was ever seen again.

Frank Hurley (1885–1962)

Hurley was born in Sydney, Australia and was working for a photographer's firm in that city when he joined Douglas Mawson's Australasian Antarctic Expedition as its official cameraman. He served in the same capacity on Shackleton's Imperial Trans-Antarctic Expedition in 1914–17. An official war photographer in both world wars, Hurley also went back to the Antarctic in 1929 as a member of the British, Australian and New Zealand Antarctic Research Expedition. Like Herbert Ponting, Hurley took some of the most memorable images from the so-called Heroic Age of Antarctic Exploration.

Frederick Jackson (1860–1938)

After travelling in Greenland and Siberia, Jackson was appointed leader of a major expedition to explore Franz Josef Land under the auspices of the Royal Geographical Society. During this expedition, he had an unlikely meeting in the Arctic wilderness with Nansen and Johansen who were struggling back from their Farthest North journey. Without Jackson's assistance it is extremely doubtful they would have made it.

Hjalmar Johansen (1867–1913)

In his twenties, Johansen joined Nansen's *Fram* expedition and was the older explorer's companion on the journey to the Farthest North in 1895. In the first decade of the twentieth century he took part in a number of smaller Arctic expeditions and was invited to join Amundsen when he took Nansen's old ship to Antarctica. Johansen quarrelled badly with his leader during the expedition and was excluded from the polar party. On his return to Norway, he fell into a severe depression, drank heavily and eventually committed suicide.

Elisha Kent Kane (1820–1857)

Kane was a US naval surgeon who was medical officer on one of the first American expeditions to travel in search of John Franklin and his men. On his return, he became a popular public lecturer, author and advocate of his nation's further involvement in Arctic exploration. He led his own expedition back to the Canadian Arctic but it ended in abandonment of his ship and an increasingly desperate journey back to safety. Kane, who suffered from poor health throughout much of his adventurous life, died in Cuba where he had gone at the suggestion of his doctor.

Carl Koldewey (1837–1908)

Like so many other polar explorers, Koldewey was a naval officer. Under the auspices of the leading geographer and cartographer August Petermann, he led two German Arctic expeditions between 1868 and 1870. Both hoped ultimately to reach the pole. Both failed, the first being driven back by ice near Spitsbergen and the second mapping parts of Greenland but again finding the ice an impassable barrier.

George F Lyon (1795–1832)

One of the few explorers who ventured into both the fierce heat of the Sahara and the freezing cold of the Arctic, Lyon was a naval officer who became a protégé of the powerful Sir John Barrow in his early twenties. He made a disastrously unsuccessful attempt to reach Timbuktu in 1818 and then, three years later, captained a ship in Parry's second expedition in search of the Northwest Passage. Lyon's own Arctic expedition the following year was another failure, largely for reasons beyond Lyon's control, and he was never given another command.

Albert Markham (1841–1918)

The younger cousin of Sir Clements Markham, the powerful President of the Royal Geographical Society, Albert Markham had a long and distinguished naval career but is best remembered today for his service in the British Arctic expedition led by George Nares. The expedition failed in its ultimate goal of reaching the North Pole but Markham's sledging trip to a Farthest North of 83° 20′ set a new record.

Douglas Mawson (1882–1958)

An Australian geologist, Mawson travelled with Shackleton's *Nimrod* expedition of 1907–09 and was amongst the party that was the first to reach the South Magnetic Pole. After refusing an invitation to join Scott's *Terra Nova* expedition, he organised his own Australasian Antarctic expedition which worked on the continent between 1911 and 1914. He was also the leader of the British Australian and New Zealand Antarctic Research Expedition of 1929–31.

Francis McClintock (1819–1907)

McClintock was already an experienced Arctic traveller who had been on several expeditions and surveyed many miles of hitherto uncharted coastline when he was picked by Lady Jane Franklin to command the *Fox* which set off in 1857 to search for clues as to the fate of her missing husband. In 1859, McClintock's expedition came across both written evidence of what had happened to Franklin and a boat containing the skeletons of two of his men.

Robert McClure (1807–1873)

After sailing as an officer on James Clark Ross's expedition of 1848–49 to search for Franklin and his men, McClure returned to the Arctic in command of HMS *Investigator* which sailed through the Bering Strait and into the Arctic Ocean from the west. *Investigator* had to be abandoned in 1853 and, after travelling by sledge across the ice, McClure and his men were rescued and taken to a ship which had entered the Arctic from the east. They thus became, in effect, the first men to traverse a Northwest Passage from the Pacific to the Atlantic.

Fridtjof Nansen (1861–1930)

Nansen was a scientist who took up exploration after studies in zoology and neurobiology. Following a trans-Greenland expedition in 1888, he devised a plan to reach the pole by taking advantage of the natural drift of the ice. His ship *Fram* began its drift across the top of the world but, after more than a year in the ice, it became clear that it would not cross the pole. Together with one companion, Hjalmar Johansen, Nansen left the *Fram* in an attempt to make it to the pole on foot. They failed to do so but reached 86° 13' before admitting defeat. After a death-defying retreat southwards they met the English explorer Frederick Jackson on Franz Josef Land and were rescued. Nansen never returned to exploration but became a highly respected statesman and humanitarian who won the

Nobel Peace Prize for his work with refugees after the First World War.

George Nares (1831–1915)

After joining the navy as a teenager, Nares was a junior officer on one of the Franklin search expeditions in the early 1850s. In 1874 he was in command of the HMS *Challenger* in its extended scientific voyage around the world's oceans when he was recalled to take charge of the British Arctic Expedition of 1875–76 which made an unsuccessful attempt to reach the North Pole.

Umberto Nobile (1885–1978)

An Italian engineer who was fascinated by the airship and its potential, Nobile had already designed and flown several such craft when he was approached by Roald Amundsen and asked to create one which could travel to the North Pole. The result was the *Norge* on which Amundsen, Nobile and others flew to the pole in 1926. Two years later, during a further flight to the pole and back on the *Italia*, another airship he had designed, Nobile crash-landed. He and the men who had survived the crash were the subjects of an international rescue mission during which Amundsen lost his life.

Adolf Nordenskjöld (1832–1901)

A scientist and politician as well as an explorer, Adolf Nordenskjöld made a series of journeys in the Scandinavian and Russian Arctic in the 1860s and 1870s. In 1878–79, aboard the Swedish steamship SS *Vega*, he led the first expedition to sail through the Northeast Passage. He was the uncle of the Antarctic explorer Otto Nordenskjöld.

Otto Nordenskjöld (1869–1928)

A professor of geology at Uppsala University and nephew of a famous polar explorer, Otto Nordenskjöld led the Swedish

Antarctic Expedition of 1901–04. He also travelled in Greenland and Alaska but, after braving the wildernesses of the Arctic and the Antarctic, he met his death on a street in the Swedish city of Gothenburg when he was knocked down by a bus.

Lawrence Oates (1880–1912)
A cavalry officer in the 6th Inniskilling Dragoons, Oates was taken on Scott's *Terra Nova* expedition to look after the ponies that were expected to play a significant role in the transport to the pole. He was one of the four men who accompanied Scott to the South Pole, only to find that Amundsen had been there before them. On the return journey, Oates, suffering from frostbite and gangrene and aware that he was holding back his comrades, walked out of the tent to certain death with the famous last words, 'I am just going outside and may be some time'.

Erasmus Ommanney (1814–1904)
A long-serving navy officer who had experience of Arctic waters, Ommanney was chosen to take part in the early Admiralty-sponsored searches for Franklin. In August 1850, he captained the ship which landed at Beechey Island and found the remains of Franklin's first winter camp.

Nathaniel Palmer (1799–1877)
Palmer was a Connecticut seal hunter who sailed south of Cape Horn in 1820. He and the men on board his ship the *Hero* became the first Americans to sight the Antarctic continent. Palmer Land on the Antarctic Peninsula is named after him.

William Parry (1790–1855)
Parry first went to the Arctic as an officer in John Ross's expedition of 1818. He returned on four more occasions as leader of his own expeditions. Although he was unsuccessful in finding the elusive Northwest Passage and lost one of his ships

on his third expedition, Parry charted large areas of the Canadian Arctic and was one of the most successful polar explorers of the first half of the nineteenth century. On his last expedition, in 1827, he made one of the first concerted efforts to reach the North Pole. It failed but he made it to 82° 45' N, the farthest north recorded for nearly fifty years.

Julius von Payer (1841–1915)

A soldier who had served with distinction in the Austro-Prussian War of 1866, Payer was also a well-known mountaineer and Alpinist. Because of his experiences in the Alps, he was invited to join Carl Koldewey's second German polar expedition of 1869–70. After his return, he joined forces with Karl Weyprecht to mount two Austro-Hungarian expeditions in the Arctic. The first went to Novaya Zemlya; the second discovered an archipelago in the Far North which was named Franz Josef Land, after the Austro-Hungarian emperor.

Josephine Peary (1863–1955)

Born in Maryland, Josephine Diebitsch married Robert Peary in 1888. She accompanied her husband on several of his expeditions and was the first western woman to travel in the Arctic. In 1893, with the arrival in the world of Marie Peary, she also became the first western woman to give birth in the Far North.

Robert E Peary (1856–1920)

Peary travelled in the Arctic for the first time in 1886, when he trekked into the interior of Greenland, and spent the next twenty years and more in pursuit of his ultimate goal – the North Pole. Between 1891 and 1905 he organised and led four expeditions to the Arctic. On his fifth such expedition in 1908-09, he claimed to have reached the pole with Matthew Henson and a group of four Inuit hunters. On his return to the USA, he found himself embroiled in a furious controversy with Frederick Cook who said he had reached the pole a year before Peary. Peary won the contest with Cook and was acclaimed as the first man to reach the North Pole but the consensus today is that he did no more than make it to a point close to the pole.

Herbert Ponting (1870–1935)
Many of the most iconic images of Antarctic exploration, including the one that forms the cover of this book, are the work of Herbert Ponting who was the official photographer and cinematographer on Scott's *Terra Nova* expedition. Born in Wiltshire, Ponting had worked as a Californian fruit farmer before earning his living as a globe-trotting traveller, taking pictures of exotic places for books and magazines. In his darkroom in one of the huts at Scott's base camp, he produced more than 1000 photographs recording the expedition.

John Rae (1813–1893)
A Scottish doctor who worked for the Hudson's Bay Company, Rae made extensive journeys around the Gulf of Boothia in Canada's Far North in the years 1846 and 1847. A few years later he undertook a series of journeys in search of information about the fate of Sir John Franklin and his men. Some of the evidence he gathered from the Inuit, particularly reports of starving sailors resorting to cannibalism, was greeted with horror and disbelief back in Britain.

Knud Rasmussen (1879–1933)
Born in Greenland, Rasmussen devoted his life to learning more about the geography of his native land and the culture of its peoples. He organised a series of expeditions known as the Thule expeditions between 1912 and his death.

John Richardson (1787–1865)
Naval surgeon John Richardson travelled on Franklin's disastrous Coppermine Expedition in the early 1820s and was central to its

most controversial incident when he killed one of its members whom he suspected of murder and cannibalism. He returned with Franklin to the Canadian Arctic a few years later in a much more successful expedition and travelled with John Rae on a journey to search for his old comrade in 1848–49.

Alfred Ritscher (1879–1963)

A captain in the German Navy, Ritscher was already approaching his sixtieth birthday in 1938 when the Nazi regime began planning an expedition to Antarctica. However, he was one of the few serving officers with any polar experience – he had travelled on a small expedition to the Arctic just before the First World War – and he was appointed to command the *Schwabenland* on its voyage to the Far South. From its decks, small planes flew across areas of the continent which were claimed as German territory.

Edith Ronne (1919–2009)

Wife of Finn Ronne, she became the first woman to set foot on the Antarctic continent and the first to overwinter there when she took part in her husband's expedition of 1946–48. The Ronne Ice Shelf was originally known as Edith Ronne Land.

Finn Ronne (1899–1980)

Born in Norway, Ronne became a US citizen at the end of the 1920s. He was an important member of several of Richard Byrd's expeditions to the Antarctic in the 1930s and led the Ronne Antarctic Research Expedition after the Second World War. He continued to be a major figure in US Antarctic research until his death.

James Clark Ross (1800–1862)

The nephew of John Ross, with whom he often had a difficult and argumentative relationship, James Clark Ross served on a series of Arctic expeditions in the 1820s and 1830s. In 1831, during his uncle's second expedition, he became the first man to reach the North Magnetic Pole. Between 1839 and 1843, Ross commanded the two ships HMS *Terror* and HMS *Erebus* on an expedition to Antarctica which discovered the sea named after him and charted stretches of the continent's icy coastline. In 1848, he commanded one of the earliest expeditions to search unsuccessfully for the missing Franklin expedition.

John Ross (1777–1856)
An officer who had served in the navy since he was a boy, Ross was chosen by Sir John Barrow at the Admiralty to command a new journey in search of the Northwest Passage in 1818. Although he was severely criticised after his first expedition for his unwillingness to explore further than he did, he became one of the most experienced of all Arctic voyagers in the nineteenth century. During his second expedition, he was forced to spend four winters amidst the ice. At the time of his third expedition in 1850, in search of his old colleague John Franklin, Ross was a man in his seventies. He was the uncle of fellow explorer James Clark Ross.

John Riddoch Rymill (1905–1968)
An Australian who studied in London, Rymill was a member of two expeditions led by Gino Watkins and organised the British Graham Land expedition of 1934–37, which was one of the last Antarctic expeditions to be largely financed by private sponsors rather than government.

Otto Schmidt (1891–1956)
Born into a family of German descent in what is now Belarus, Schmidt became a leading figure in Soviet science and a well-known Arctic explorer. In the early 1930s, when he was head of his country's Arctic Institute, he participated in or led a series of expeditions to Franz Josef Land and through the Northeast Passage.

Robert Falcon Scott (1868–1912)

Scott was working as a lieutenant on a torpedo boat when he was persuaded by his mentor Sir Clements Markham to apply to become leader of a recently announced expedition to Antarctica. He got the job and took the *Discovery* south to McMurdo Sound between 1901 and 1904. With Wilson and Shackleton, he undertook a sledge journey to what was then the Farthest South of 82° 17'. He returned to the Antarctic in 1910 on the *Terra Nova*, with the avowed intention of reaching the South Pole. Together with four companions, he arrived at his goal in January 1912 only to find that the Norwegian Roald Amundsen had been there a month earlier. On the increasingly desperate march back towards their base, all the men lost their lives. Trapped by blizzards in a tent only a few miles from a food depot, Scott may well have been the last to die, perhaps on 29 March, the day that he made his last entry in his diary.

Georgy Sedov (1877–1914)

Born into poverty in a small Russian village, Sedov escaped his background through luck and intelligence and became an officer in the Tsarist Navy. After serving in the Russo-Japanese War of 1904–05, he embarked on a series of explorations and expeditions in Franz Josef Land and other islands in the Russian Arctic. He died during an over-ambitious attempt to reach the North Pole.

Ernest Shackleton (1874–1922)

Born in Ireland and educated at Dulwich College, London, Shackleton served as an officer in the Merchant Navy before joining Scott's *Discovery* expedition and embarking on the career that made him one of the most famous of all polar explorers. Invalided home after the Farthest South trip with Scott and Wilson in 1903, he returned to lead his own expedition to Antarctica a few years later and reached a point within 100 miles of the South Pole in January 1909 before being forced to turn back. He led the Imperial Trans-Antarctic Expedition of 1914–17 during which he took part in an epic boat journey to South Georgia to seek help for his men stranded on an uninhabited island in the Southern Ocean. He died of a heart attack while leading his final expedition to Antarctica.

Nobu Shirase (1861–1946)

The son of a Buddhist priest, Shirase joined the Japanese army as a young man. He took part in a disastrous expedition to the Kuril Islands, north of his country, in the 1880s and fought in the Russo–Japanese War in 1904–05. With little encouragement or financial assistance from the government, he organised the Japanese Antarctic expedition of 1910–12.

Vilhjalmur Stefansson (1879–1962)

Born in Canada to parents who had emigrated from Iceland, Stefansson made several voyages in the Arctic before leading one of the most catastrophic and controversial expeditions in polar history. During the Canadian Arctic Expedition of 1913–16, eleven men lost their lives and Stefansson was accused of abandoning his responsibilities when he left the expedition's main ship, the *Karluk*, at a time it was trapped in the ice. He defended his actions and continued his career as an Arctic explorer in the 1920s.

Otto Sverdrup (1854–1930)

Sverdrup was a sea captain who had known Fridtjof Nansen for some years when the young Norwegian scientist and explorer invited him to join an expedition across Greenland. He went on to become second in command of Nansen's *Fram* expedition between 1893 and 1896. When Nansen and Johansen left the ship in their attempt to reach the North Pole, Sverdrup was left in charge of the ship and brought it home to Norway. He led two expeditions of his own to the Arctic in 1914 and 1921.

George Vancouver (1757–1798)

The man after whom the great Canadian city of Vancouver was named was born in King's Lynn, Norfolk and joined the navy at the age of fifteen. He served as a midshipman on both the second and the third voyage of Captain Cook and later conducted his own extensive surveys of the north-west coast of America which he had first visited with Cook.

Gino Watkins (1907–1932)

Henry George 'Gino' Watkins first travelled to the Arctic as a Cambridge undergraduate in 1927. Three years later he led the British Arctic Air Route Expedition to Greenland which aimed to explore unknown areas on the proposed course of flights between the UK and the US via the Arctic. When a planned expedition to Antarctica fell through in 1932, Watkins returned to Greenland and disappeared during a solo seal hunting trip.

James Weddell (1787–1834)

James Weddell was an experienced sailor with a taste for exploration when he undertook a series of voyages in Antarctic waters between 1819 and 1824. Ostensibly, his purpose was to hunt the seals that abounded there but he was as much interested in discovery of new lands as he was in hunting. In February 1823, he sailed further south than anyone had gone before in the sea that was later given his name.

Karl Weyprecht (1838–1881)

Weyprecht was an officer in the Austro-Hungarian navy who, together with Julius von Payer, undertook a journey to the Russian Arctic in 1871 and, from 1872–74, led the North Pole expedition which discovered Franz Josef Land. Weyprecht was one of the prime movers behind the First International Polar Year but died of tuberculosis before he could see his plans reach fruition.

Frank Wild (1873–1939)

A Yorkshire-born seaman who served on Scott's *Discovery* expedition, Wild is best known as a close associate of Ernest Shackleton. He was one of the group that reached the Farthest South during Shackleton's *Nimrod* expedition and served as second in command on the Imperial Trans-Antarctic Expedition between 1914 and 1916. When Shackleton made his heroic boat journey to South Georgia, Wild was left in charge of the men stranded on Elephant Island. He was also second in command on Shackleton's last expedition in 1921–22.

Charles Wilkes (1798–1877)

Wilkes was a naval officer who commanded the United States Exploring Expedition which made two significant journeys into Antarctic waters in 1839 and 1840. He sighted the Antarctic continent on several occasions and part of it is still named after him.

Hubert Wilkins (1888–1958)

Born in South Australia, Wilkins travelled on several polar expeditions and served as an aviator in the First World War before organising his own expedition in 1928 to make pioneering flights in the Arctic. He turned his attention to the Antarctic later in the same year and carried out a series of aerial explorations. His *Nautilus* expedition of 1931 was a failed attempt to take a submarine under the Arctic ice.

Edward Wilson (1872–1912)

Wilson was born in Cheltenham and educated at Cambridge. His training as a doctor was interrupted by illness but he completed his studies and qualified in 1900. He joined the *Discovery* expedition a year later and became Scott's closest confidant, accompanying him and Shackleton on the Farthest South journey. He was chief of the scientific staff on the *Terra Nova* expedition, led the winter journey to Cape Crozier and travelled to the pole. He died in the tent with Bowers and Scott on the return journey.

Oscar Wisting (1871–1936)

A gunner in the Norwegian navy, Wisting was asked by Roald Amundsen to join him on his Antarctic expedition of 1910–12 and was one of the four men who were with his leader when he reached the South Pole in December 1911. He later served with Amundsen on the *Maud* and was with him when he reached the North Pole in the airship *Norge*. Thus, together with Amundsen, Wisting was one of the first two men who could claim to have been at both the poles.

Bibliography

The bibliography of polar exploration is vast and grows vaster each year. These are just the most notable of the books I have found useful in my reading on the subject and the ones that I think would most benefit readers in search of more information than I could provide within the confines of a short history:

Beattie, Owen and Geiger, John, *Frozen in Time: The Fate of the Franklin Expedition*, London: Bloomsbury, 1987

Berton, Pierre, *The Arctic Grail: The Quest for the Northwest Passage and the North Pole 1818–1909*, London: Viking, 1988

Bown, Stephen, *The Last Viking: The Extraordinary Life of Roald Amundsen*, London: Aurum Press, 2012

Brandt, Anthony, *The Man Who Ate His Boots: Sir John Franklin and the Tragic History of the Northwest Passage*, London: Jonathan Cape, 2011

Cherry-Garrard, Apsley, *The Worst Journey in the World*, London: Penguin, 1970 (first published in 1922)

Crane, David, *Scott of the Antarctic*, London: HarperCollins, 2005

Day, David, *Antarctica: A Biography*, Oxford: Oxford University Press, 2013

Fiennes, Ranulph, *Captain Scott*, London: Hodder, 2003

Fleming, Fergus, *Barrow's Boys*, London: Granta, 1998

Fleming, Fergus, *Ninety Degrees North*, London: Granta, 2001

Henderson, Bruce, *True North: Peary, Cook and the Race to the Pole*, New York: WW Norton, 2005

Holland, Clive (ed.), *Farthest North: A History of North Polar*

Exploration in Eye-Witness Accounts, London: Robinson, 1994

Huntford, Roland, *Scott and Amundsen*, London: Hodder, 1979

Huntford, Roland, *Shackleton*, London: Hodder, 1985

Nansen, Fridtjof, *Farthest North*, London: Duckworth, 2000 (first published in 1897)

Riffenburgh, Beau, *Nimrod: Ernest Shackleton and the Extraordinary Story of the 1907–09 British Antarctic Expedition*, London: Bloomsbury, 2004

Riffenburgh, Beau, *Racing with Death: Douglas Mawson, Antarctic Explorer*, London: Bloomsbury, 2008

Scott, Robert Falcon, *Journals: Captain Scott's Last Expedition*, Oxford: Oxford University Press, 2005

Shackleton, Ernest, *South: The Story of Shackleton's Last Expedition 1914–17*, London: Century, 1986 (first published in 1919)

Solomon, Susan, *The Coldest March: Scott's Fatal Antarctic Expedition*, New Haven: Yale University Press, 2001

Spufford, Francis, *I May Be Some Time: Ice and the English Imagination*, London: Faber, 1996

Turney, Chris, *1912: The Year the World Discovered Antarctica*, London: Bodley Head, 2012

Williams, Glyn, *Arctic Labyrinth: The Quest for the Northwest Passage*, London: Allen Lane, 2009

Williams, Glyn, *Voyages of Delusion: The Search for the Northwest Passage in the Age of Reason*, London: HarperCollins, 2002

Index

Also available from Pocket Essentials

A Short History of China
The turbulent and chequered past of the world's most populous country is one of the most fascinating in world history, and relatively little known in the West. From the beginnings of Chinese prehistory, right through to the internet censorship of the 'Great Firewall of China', Gordon Kerr offers a comprehensive introduction to more than 4,000 years of the tyrants, despots, femmes fatales, artists, warriors and philosophers who have shaped this complex nation.

£7.99

ISBN: 978-1-84243-968-5

A Short History Africa
Africa. The cradle of civilisation. From the dawn of human time in prehistoric Africa right through to the so-called 'Arab Spring' of 2011, Gordon Kerr offers a comprehensive introduction to the sprawling history of this enormous continent. From the origins of the human race and the development of stone age technology, to the rise and fall of Africa's great nation states and kingdoms, to the colonization, exploitation and oppression of the 'Scramble for Africa'.

£7.99

ISBN: 978-1-84243-442-0

A Short History Europe
What is Europe? Firstly, of course, it is a continent made up of countless disparate peoples, races and nations, and governed by different ideas, philosophies, religions and attitudes. Nonetheless, it has a common thread of history running through it, stitching the lands and peoples of its past and present together into one fabric. Gordon Kerr follows Europe's past through from the rise of its oldest and greatest institutions, to the victories and defeats its most terrible conquerors.

£7.99

ISBN: 978-1-84243-346-1

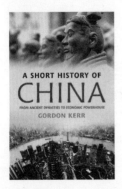 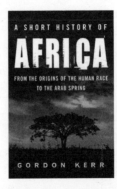 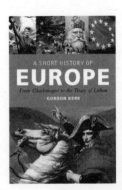